Hi Marcus!

Thought I'd send along a copy of our CEO's book.

Best,

Ben

What Works

What Works

Robert Cornish
Wil Seabrook

WILEY

John Wiley & Sons, Inc.

Published by John Wiley & Sons, Inc., Hoboken, New Jersey.
Published simultaneously in Canada.

For general information on our other products and services or for technical support, please contact our Customer Care Department within the United States at (800) 762-2974, outside the United States at (317) 572-3993 or fax (317) 572-4002.

Wiley publishes in a variety of print and electronic formats and by print-on-demand. Some material included with standard print versions of this book may not be included in e-books or in print-on-demand. If this book refers to media such as a CD or DVD that is not included in the version you purchased, you may download this material at http://booksupport.wiley.com. For more information about Wiley products, visit www.wiley.com.

Library of Congress Cataloging-in-Publication Data:

Cornish, Robert.
    What works / Robert Cornish and Wil Seabrook.
      p.   cm.
    ISBN 978-1-118-39169-3 (cloth); ISBN 978-1-118-41201-5 (ebk);
    ISBN 978-1-118-41202-2 (ebk); ISBN 978-1-118-49146-1 (ebk)
      1. Entrepreneurship. 2. Strategic planning. 3. Industrial management.
    I. Seabrook, Wil. II. Title.
    HB615.C657   2012
    658—dc23
                                                                2012012431

Printed in the United States of America

10 9 8 7 6 5 4 3 2 1

Contents

v

Preface

With most business books, you open the cover and read the introduction, which says something along these lines: "I wanted to create a book to help others with . . ." or "I'm writing this book to show people how to . . ." In my case, I wrote this book because I didn't want to forget all of the valuable things I have learned through actual experience. While writing down the information I personally have found to be true and useful (and wanted to have written down so that I can manage and run my companies better), I realized that these lessons and information could be converted into a book that I could sell as well. After all, if I find this valuable, most likely others will, too. So there you have it: honesty. Refreshing, isn't it?

This book is composed of my notes on business—what works. I wrote it down so that I wouldn't forget and turned it into a book that I could carry with me. You might benefit from doing the same. This is a book about what works in business.

Introduction

Although there are thousands of business books, tips, and articles out there, I think you would agree with me when I say that most of them are fluff—a lot of trendy concepts but very few hard-won ideas, based on actual experience, that have true applicability in the real world. You read business books because you're looking for answers. I know; I'm the same way. I've read hundreds of them—and continue to read them—out of a sheer craving for knowledge and a desire to be better, to fine-tune, and to glean a few great ideas and put them into application. But in all that searching, very few books have offered what I'm looking for.

I'd much rather just have a successful entrepreneur sit down and answer questions about what they did, how they did it, and how it turned out. That's the type of material I believe we are all looking for. I wrote this book not because I wanted to write a book, but because I made a habit from day one of taking diligent notes while starting and then growing my agency—from two partners, two phones, two computers, and two desks to 53 employees, multimillion dollar revenues, and four major component parts to our company that have resulted in more than 400 percent annual growth. I wrote down notes as soon as we did something that was successful to keep a memo for myself to review later. I took notes when we did things that were unsuccessful so we would never do them again, allowing us to quickly and thoroughly course correct.

So this book is made up of my notes based on successful and, sometimes more important, unsuccessful actions—raw data that are real, applicable, and authentic. It offers real-world applicability that we know works based on our experience in the trenches rather than high-level business theories that might or might not be proved. There is no discussion of latest trends about "fail forward" or any other silly concept; this book is truly about what works, what has worked, and what will work in the real world. It's 100 percent applicable to the challenges you're dealing with right now. This book is for any businessperson looking to grab ideas and successful actions that can be applied. It's for the entrepreneur who is looking to grow his or her company or needs a few insights for what other successful entrepreneurs have done. It's for anyone in business looking to gain an edge by getting inside, real, and applicable information that he or she can put into action today to improve his or her business—right now.

We started out in 2008 as a two-person agency focused on handling the problem of gaining attention and interest to help drive business for our clients. We felt and still feel that traditional marketing, advertising, and public relations (PR) methods and companies have failed to attain these goals for their clients in an efficient manner that provides strong results measurably improving growth and sales. We set out to change that with a new kind of agency.

We tend to look at things differently at our company. We're obsessed with having an impact—driving sales and bottom-line numbers through our efforts—because at the end of the day, not much matters in a business if you can't accomplish that. Whether you have a great idea, product, service, or business model, none of it means anything if you don't know how to drive the business forward, feeding a strong, steady flow of new clients into the company to service them effectively. So we focus on the entry point for every business across the planet—the front door. At this stage we have clients whose revenues range from $10 million to several billion dollars that rely on our agency to help them drive their business forward. It's a concept we've adopted as our basic purpose: to be mission critical to our clients' companies.

So that is what you can expect from this book—real, applicable knowledge that is not fluffed up. It's simple, to the point, and easy to read. We're not trying to be supersophisticated or use "expert" terminology that makes us sound brilliant. I want this book to help you attain your goals, so we wrote it from the viewpoint of making it easy to read, digest, and use. I wrote it the way I would want to read it. I have a few favorite books myself, and they tend to be short, simple, and punchy with great insights that can be applied. This book is another one for that collection. I'm personally going to read and reread it—these are my notes on the most workable solutions we've discovered and it's vital that we have this incorporated into our agency at all times. I'm going to have all of our people read this book because I want them to understand how we think and operate. This is made up of what we actually use, and it has resulted in our company becoming one of the fastest growing companies in America. My hope is that it does the same for you.

What Works

On Sales

Care

It's a simple concept but few recognize it or actually apply it to sales or business in general: care. You have to care about your prospects. Care about your clients. Care to be interested. No, not the fake kind that comes across as awkwardness on the receiving end. I'm talking about the authentic kind. Actually be interested in your prospects and clients. Ask questions. Take some time to study their sites to clearly understand their companies and where they may need help and where you may fit in.

Too many salespeople clearly care about only one thing: their commission to fatten their pockets. The truth is, that is the longest and hardest route you could take. Instead, focus on genuinely caring about your prospects. There is a reason, purpose, or need that they are trying to handle or resolve, which is why they called you. Care to find out what that reason or purpose is. Understand it. Ask questions. Problem solve with them to help manage it. Get excited about them and their company and focus on helping them attain their goals faster. Be genuine and care. This is your fastest route to actually making a sale.

It's difficult to express this one factor in writing; all I can really tell you is that you have to care genuinely about prospects and clients enough to be truly interested in them and focused on helping them. Care enough to have engaging dialog, even if it goes off track, leading to topics such as family, travel, or life—care to listen, care to be interested, and care to genuinely help. Believe me, it will come across to your prospects and they will love you for it. It will also make your job and your day that much more interesting. You want faster sales? This is the way. Care.

Pipeline Comes before Sales

While discussing the importance of talented salespeople with my partner, the conversation turned to that critical element of the sales process that comes before sales and that most people neglect: developing sales opportunities.

If you head to a local bookstore today, you'll find many books on selling, sales technique, sales motivation, best practices, and so on, but you will rarely find a book about successful methods for developing strong interest from the correct audience to create the initial sales opportunity.

Having trained and competent salespeople is obviously vital for any company, but don't neglect the sales prospecting actions to fill their pipeline. You can have the greatest salesperson in the world working for you, but if you lack people to sell to, the salesperson is wasted. Focus a huge amount of your efforts on driving new prospective clients to your sales team so that they can work their magic and do what they should be doing: selling and closing new business. You can never have too much in the pipeline, so jam it full of new prospects.

Sales, Selling, and Getting Your People to Sell

What role does sales play in your company? Have you recognized the fact that every person and every opportunity provides another angle to sell? Let me clarify. Sales is intertwined into every aspect of your company.

You need to sell your products and services to your target market. You then need to sell and keep selling your own people internally on the value of your company, on the task at hand, and on your new clients, which motivates them to get the job done and carry forward what was sold. You then need to get people in your company to sell to your clients, your prospective public, and other employees to constantly carry your company forward.

Although there are many posts and titles in any company, everyone has a role in selling. A smile to a new client walking through the door sells. A welcome e-mail to a new client sells. A follow-up call to a client sells. Everyone in the company plays a role in selling either to cultivate new business, to cater to and maintain current clients to ensure they are happy and are constantly sold on your company, or to keep the team focused and motivated. The executive team, managers, and the chief executive officer (CEO) alike all sell the people of the company on the goals, future, mission at hand, and their specific tasks to motivate people to get the job done. Sales is a vital and central part of your company and is by no means isolated to simply bringing in new business. It is, after all, simply earning someone else's agreement with your viewpoint.

Keep this closely in mind and review every aspect of your company if you want to stay competitive and grow your organization. Lose sight of this, and you will lose the game. Sales is a companywide sport. It takes a team approach, and everyone must be aware of the rules of the game.

Saying No and Walking Away

There is a saying in business that goes like this: "Sometimes the best deal is the one you didn't make." In other words, it's the deal you turned away or left on the table that saved you money, time, and your sanity in the long run. It's always tempting to take on every single deal that comes your way in business due to the lure of possible profits related to it, but I would advise you to look closely at every deal to ensure that the prospect fits your criteria and that the deal will truly be profitable for you.

This may mean that if something doesn't feel right about a deal, the prospect is being difficult at the outset, or it's outside of your core competency, then you may need to get up and walk away from it for the sake of your company. It most likely will be for the best, saving you and your company huge amounts of wasted time and effort, not to mention money.

One of the most profitable angles in business is knowing who your target public (or audience) is and who is a desirable client to take on and who isn't. If you can peg who isn't, you will avoid 90 percent of all headaches for your company. The ability to spot problem children early is a vital tool toward a growing and profitable company. Sure, you may end up leaving a few perfectly good deals on the table, but you don't need to worry about that. Focus on isolating the deals that don't fully align with your goals, purposes, and policies; I assure you that by doing so, you will ultimately be more profitable and much happier.

I have found that the very clients who fall just outside of our core public in one way or another try to actually sell us on taking them on when all of our instincts and observations are indicating that we shouldn't. Every time we have violated our polices and our instincts we have ended up unhappy about it later, so my advice is save yourself the headaches and weed out the possible problem clients early. Don't be reasonable about this. Be ruthless about it. There are absolute hordes of new business out there; why waste your time with the deadwood?

If you currently have problem clients who fall outside of your core public or don't qualify in one way or the other, do yourself a favor and resign them. Move them off the line and focus all of your best talent, time, and energy on your key clients to ensure they are happy and being serviced well. Take good care of your qualified clients and work to add more just like them. Do this, and you will see the overall morale of your company improve. At our agency, we try to take on clients who fit our target public exactly and have products or services we like. We also try to work only with people we like, and if a client is difficult or rude to our people, we simply resign the account and move onward and upward. Give it a try. It can be very liberating and empowering, and it will ultimately speed your expansion and success.

The Art of the Follow-up

These days people are busy . . . busier than ever. This isn't to say they are more productive than ever, just busier. They are on iPhones, checking Facebook, downloading apps, juggling work tasks and projects, trying to keep their heads above the ocean of e-mails, handling personal problems, dealing with company problems, and the list goes on.

Call it dispersed or distracted or even disorganized, but whatever the case, your communication to these busy people is not impinging or getting a response. Before you get too discouraged, realize that these same daily distractions are diverting your message and causing chaos, which is part of the reason you are not getting a response.

Too often I see salespeople burn deals they are working on simply because they have "followed up," not received a response, and therefore assumed the deal to be cold or dead. Although this seems logical, it isn't. You must keep clearly in mind the ever-present reality that people are busy and easily distracted.

Your job is to be organized for yourself and your prospect, to follow up diligently over and over in order to stay on the prospect's radar, and to continue to interest the prospect until you have received a response and can move the deal forward.

You can follow up by phone, e-mail, LinkedIn messages or connection request, Skype, Facebook, Twitter, or anything else. Just focus on (politely) getting yourself in front of the prospect to remind him or her of your dialog until a commitment is made to devote some time and energy to whatever it is that you want to discuss or propose.

I apply this approach and consistently receive comments of appreciation for my diligent follow-up because, without it, the prospect would have forgotten and moved on to one of the zillion other tasks being juggled. I don't say this to toot my own horn but rather to point out that although it may sometimes seem like the prospect is not interested, the person may simply be too busy or distracted to respond. So always be diligent and follow up until your prospect is ready to discuss; this will dramatically improve your sales.

The Sales Team's Role

Out of all of the actions your business development team or sales team should be working on, attempting to find new business and/or prospecting is not one of them—that is, not if you want to increase production and sales. Every person is different, including salespeople. They have different methods for going about things and how they manage, work, and produce. I haven't seen one salesperson who has a steady method of developing consistent new business. Salespeople need to focus on selling and closing new business, as well as on following up and catering to current clients who potentially will purchase again.

The vital daily and weekly tasks of a salesperson should include:

- Handling new prospects to sell
- Making phone calls or scheduling meetings
- Traveling to meetings
- Following up with prospects or clients

- E-mailing or writing letters to prospects
- Creating and sending proposals
- Closing deals

Prospecting to develop new potential clients should be done either by a separate unit within your company that supports sales or by an agency. It's unproductive to have your sales team spend their time trying to find and develop new prospective clients with methods that may or may not work, because it results in lost sales opportunities with the people in their current pipeline. The truth is, most salespeople are not very good at it and don't really like it anyway.

By using internal resources to maintain a very full pipeline or hiring an agency to do so, you will improve productivity and cut out wasted efforts for your team. Focus on filling their pipeline with qualified new prospective business and keeping it full so that they can spend their time selling and closing new business. It will make your salespeople happy, and you'll ultimately be happy as well since this will certainly increase your profits.

The Tough Part of Sales

Making your company's products or services known to the correct target public to gain interest and reach has traditionally been the most difficult part of sales. How do your prospective clients find out about your company? How do you make the initial contact or the initial introduction to cultivate interest?

Times have changed. The things that used to work— going to companies door to door to get an appointment or cold-calling a specific prospect to try to get 2 minutes of their time—are not as effective as they once were. New rules of business etiquette have interrupted these strategies. People are busy and don't want to be interrupted by uninvited visitors or random phone calls.

We have experienced over and over that the name of the game is relationships and making smart introductions to the right people. The online world and, more specifically, new media have created an avenue to replace old systems of making introductions and building relationships with new ways that are generally acceptable in this day and age.

You don't have to e-mail blast 1,000 people to hope for a response rate of 1 to 2 percent; you need to make only one connection—one introduction to the right person with the right message to penetrate and gain interest and reach.

The methods of reaching out to prospective clients and making your company a known quantity as well as sparking interest have changed. Successfully adopted and used correctly, they will dramatically change your sales as well. Again I refer you back to the new media equivalent of the Golden Rule: send only the exact type of communication that you yourself, as a busy executive, would like to receive. Always remember, there is another "you" on the receiving end of every communication.

Asking

Since our agency is completely focused on business development, relationships, and ultimately sales, we end up studying and discussing the topic frequently. This then brings up the topic of asking and its importance in sales.

You can do virtually everything exactly "right" in a sales cycle, but if you don't ask, you won't close. It's that simple. It's so ridiculously simple that it's one of those things that it seems everyone should know, do, and apply, but most don't. I've had plenty of people attempt to sell me products or services and never ask me, which invariably results in me not buying. I'm sure you have as well.

Think it over. On your last sales cycle, did you clearly ask for the sale? If so, how many times? If not, why not? People seem to hesitate when it comes time to ask for the sale. It seems to be an awkward moment for all involved, but if you practice it enough and do it enough, it becomes second nature. Many sales cycles seem to go very well—the prospect is interested, you have a great discussion, the person needs or wants what you are selling—and yet the deal doesn't close. You follow up and still the deal doesn't close. Perhaps the follow-up goes something like this: "Hi, did you get my proposal I sent over? . . . Great . . . well . . . I was just following up with you . . . mmmm hmmm . . . Okay . . . any questions? . . . Great . . . Okay, I will follow up next week . . . " If you don't ask, you won't close. It's that simple.

Ask as many times as it takes to close the deal. If you ask once and the answer is something like, "We still need to look at . . . ," no problem. Don't take it personally; handle that point and then . . . you guessed it . . . ask again. Ask and ask and ask until it's done while handling any objections and concerns along the way. Don't back off. The client has an interest and wants to buy the product. In fact, you do your prospect a favor by asking and closing the deal. People are not very good at selling and closing themselves. A skilled salesperson who is an expert at selling, asking, and closing business is actually a pleasure to deal with. It's the ones who drag their feet, are hesitant, and can't control the cycle that cause the awkwardness associated with the sale.

Here is what I want you to do: for any deal you are working on, try asking for the sale this week. Just ask your prospect. Come right out and say, "Listen, I want you to get started on this strategy this week. Let's start on this today." Or say something similar to directly ask for the sale. Trust me, this will change your sales for the better for you and your prospects. They want to be asked, so ask them!

Long Sales Pitches

Here's the deal. If it takes a long time to pitch, then in the words of Ben Affleck's character in *Good Will Hunting*, "Ya suspect."

Whether it's a long e-mail or sales letter, Web page, or video pitch, if it's too long, you're leaving money on the table. In other words, your deletion rate or rejection rate is very high. Keep it short, punchy, and sweet. Focus your message and don't waste people's time. Get to the point and concentrate on impact. You're absolutely kidding yourself if you think people will read an e-mail that's a page in content.

If it's an e-mail, keep it to a few lines with a link to where you want people to go or entice them to reach out to you for more information. If it's a video, keep it under 2 minutes. People will look at the time frame of the video and generally won't even watch it if it's much longer than 3 minutes; conversely, we have found that less than 2 minutes is powerful.

People are busy. People naturally resist sales, not to mention lengthy pitches that take up their precious time. Again, think about the kind of pitch you yourself would be willing to sit through. Sales is a strategy sport. Be brief. Cut to the point and focus on your audience's needs or wants in a short punchy way and your response rate will go way up.

If They Were Sold, It Would Be Done

Every salesperson at some point has gotten caught up in the moment and excitement of a sale, and every salesperson has also learned the painful lesson that it's not done until it's done.

So many times salespeople trick themselves into saying and believing that the deal is done. "They're sold!" says the confident salesperson. Are they? If they were sold, it would be done. Contract signed. Paperwork in the door and money in hand. Has the check cleared your account? That's sold. That's done.

If a prospect is completely and utterly sold on your offering, he or she will close immediately. If the prospect doesn't close (as in done, done, done), there is something lingering—some thought, some reservation, or doubt that must be handled to conclude the cycle and actually make the sale. Believe me, if the prospect has not signed, it's because he or she is not fully sold. Figure out what is stopping the person from signing now, handle it, sell all the way through, and then close the deal . . . today.

Decide for Them

In sales, there comes a point when you have to ask for the close in some form or fashion. This can be a somewhat awkward moment for many people. Some make common mistakes at this point and experience regret immediately after hanging up the phone or leaving the meeting, often thinking, "Oh, dammit, I should have said [insert brilliant line here]." Yes, it's happened to all of us. You get to the point of closing a deal right then and there and you ask the client to make a tough decision: "Would you like to do this or that?"

You're making your sales life harder than it needs to be. Here is what I want you to do: make the decision for your prospect. Tell, rather than ask. There's a tactful and smooth way to do this, and it works. Rather than saying, "Do you want to pay by check or corporate card?" say, "We will bill this to your corporate card and e-mail the receipt. What are the card details?" Make the decisions for your prospects so that they don't have to. Believe me, you save the prospects' time as well as your own. The prospects prefer it this way as well—fewer decisions, less hassle, fewer things to think about.

Give it a try. For any situation that may require you to ask for a decision, instead make the decision on behalf of the prospect to handle it right then and there. You will find that this speeds up the sales cycle and improves the overall close percentages, not to mention reduces work and effort for you and the prospect.

Hold Your Position

In sales, you can frequently be knocked off your position by your prospect, which can lead to no sale. What I mean by this is that sometimes the prospect will push you on a negotiation point that you attempt to handle and cater to, only to realize that this didn't close the sale.

Bending over backward and trying to cater to every request from the prospect will not close the sale. You must have the ability to hold your position and stay true to what you sell and what you can or cannot do. Use tactful communication to steer the conversation where you want it to go, and then handle objections rather than just buckling to them. It's okay to say "no." In fact, it can be an incredible negotiating and sales tool to simply say, "I'm sorry, but we can't make that work. But here is how we can address this . . . " Or simply walk away from the deal if you can't handle the concern. As strange as it may sound, you would be amazed at how walking away from a deal can be a powerful tool to actually closing the sale. Many prospects will reach back even stronger after you have walked away from the negotiating table. In other words, they are now more interested and begin to pursue the deal greater because, for some reason or other, that's how human nature works.

The key point here is to stay strong on your position. For example, if the price of an item is $1,000 and the prospect wants it for $900, you can simply say, "We can't do it for that price, but the truth is, the market price for this is $2,000 so you are already getting the best possible rate. And because you're dealing with us, we will provide a best practices guide at the end to assist you with this, which will help you dramatically improve sales from this service . . . "

With the preceding example, you hold your position while selling to the prospect and conclude the deal with a value add. Be smart about how to handle each situation and keep in mind that buckling under pressure from the prospect's demands will not help you make a sale. You're better off holding your position and using tactful communication to steer the deal toward the desired outcome.

Time to Cut the PR and Hit Them Straight

There's a point in the sales cycle when the sales pitch, song and dance, and public relations (PR) need to end and you need to come right out and hit the prospect straight. Let's say, for example, that you are selling to a prospect and you have done the dance. You have fully sold him on the product or service. You have answered his questions. There really isn't anything else to do except ask him for money. Many times, it's awkward for everyone. But, if you're good, it doesn't have to be. This is where many salespeople fail and leave deals hanging, sometimes resulting in a lost deal. They continue on too long with the sales pitch or dance around the close, making comments such as, "Hi, John, just checking in to see if anything is needed." It's just constant PR with no end in sight and it doesn't help anyone. At that point, you should come right out with a clear comment or statement that will conclude the deal such as, "John, we have talked about the service and everything is exactly what you need right now, so let's get started. Here is what I need you to do . . . " This makes it 100 percent crystal clear that you are now selling and closing the deal. Take charge of it and walk it through till it's a done deal. If the prospect is still dragging his feet, address it: "John, this is the right move, so what do we need to do to take the time out of this and get this rolling now?" Be as direct as possible without the PR hype and without trying to walk on eggshells. Don't dance around the issue. Be direct and straight and make it very clear with your question that your goal is to close the deal. I see a lot of salespeople really mess this one up by never actually getting up the confidence to be straight with the prospect. It's key to drop all sales talk or PR and simply ask for the order in the most direct fashion possible. The prospect in many cases actually needs you to do this. Prospects won't close themselves, you know. You have to do it, and in order to do it, you need to hit them straight, be direct, and come out and say exactly what you want to say in order to close the deal. Trust me: this won't blow the sale; this will close it.

Taking Money Is Good for Them

In sales, it's easy to back off from the prospect when it comes time to collect the money because it feels awkward. People do very strange things when it comes time for them to hand over the money. They may drag their feet or come up with every reason in the book why they can't do it right now. I don't know why this is, but from what I have observed, people are a little crazy on the subject of money. You can't pay any attention to this. Don't get distracted by the foot dragging, excuses, objections, and so on. Know and be confident that they got to this point because they are interested and want to buy the product or service. They just need to be handled and guided in a direct and firm manner through the process of exchanging the money so that they can get what they want and you can collect the money to close the deal. But know this: taking money from prospects is actually good for them. Once you have taken the money, here is what happens:

1. They are immediately relieved and happy that they have made a decision and now have the product or service you sold them. For example, say you are selling an $800 Apple iPad but the person is in the middle of an argument with herself ("Should I? Shouldn't I?") and begins making up all sorts of reasons why next week would be better for her or why she should think about it first. You push through this and close the deal. I can guarantee you that the second you have closed and handed her the new iPad, she will be so excited to

use it that she'll probably open the box and start playing with it on the chairs outside your store. Believe me: she won't for 1 second think about the $800 she spent. In fact, she will be happy she spent it and will probably brag to her friends that she got the "more expensive one." It's human nature. So work toward the finish line and get prospects to turn over the cash; they'll thank you for it.

2. They will immediately go into a sort of emergency mode realizing that they just spent the money and now will need to go and replenish their funds or pay off a bill to cover it. This is actually a good problem for them. People are driven by necessity. When you close a sale and take the money from the prospect, that person will now start to work toward handling that "problem" and by doing so will typically create more than the amount needed. In other words, if you closed a $5,000 deal with a prospect, he will go into emergency mode to replace the funds or cover the funds and therefore go and hustle to make it back. People are not very good at estimating the amount of effort they need to exert, so there's a pretty good chance they will overshoot what is needed and ultimately make more than what you closed them for—maybe $10,000 instead of $5,000 in this example. You'd be surprised how many times I have seen this happen. It's one of those unexplainable phenomena. Again, it's human nature.

So do your prospects a favor and push them through that awkward moment of having to take the money from them and just keep focused on the close. It's good for them. They need to spend the money because they must need or want the product or service you have. Otherwise, you wouldn't be at that stage. They require a boost of necessity to fuel their production to kick things into high gear. This is better than any motivational seminar you could send them to. And those speakers charge a fortune, so don't feel bad taking funds from your prospects—feel good about it. They will too. The product or service you are selling them has real value. The sale itself is a recognition of that, for you and for the customer.

It's Your Consideration or Theirs

There are only two things stopping any sale—I promise you that. Let's start by defining what a consideration is:

Careful thought, typically over a period of time.

So, that's all we have—a thought that moves things forward or stops things. We all know the power of the mind and thoughts. Now let's apply that same power to sales. The things to handle then are the thoughts from the prospect or the salesperson. Let's start with the salesperson. The salesperson can have thoughts that act as barriers to the sale; for example, a salesperson may think, "The price is too much for the prospect." This salesperson won't be able to close the deal. She doesn't have the confidence to pick up the phone and ask for the deal. She feels she is pestering the prospect. She doesn't want to fail, so she never tries. There are a million such thoughts that can cross the salesperson's mind, each one capable of actually stopping the sale, so you have to know with 100 percent certainty that to get the salesperson to boost sales, you have to start by managing her thoughts. From there, all other sales training, techniques, and methods can work. But without handling the negative thoughts, nothing else will work.

Then, on to the prospect. You need to handle the prospect's thoughts in order to close the deal. But first, what thoughts is he or she having? You need to become an expert at finding out what the prospect's thoughts are, and you do this by getting him or her to voice those thoughts. In other words, you need to ask questions that will get him or her talking and the questions need to be directed at getting him or her to communicate the item that is stopping the decision. This is the way to close the deal. You need to get the prospect to communicate with you so that you can ask questions to tactfully work out what thought is holding back the close. Ask questions. Get the other person talking. By engaging in dialog and asking the right questions, the prospect will eventually tell you what's causing the barrier for the sale, which then opens the door to a quick and effective handling and a closed sale in the door.

The very first thing to handle, though, is not the prospects but the salespeople. You need to ensure that they don't have thoughts that are hindering the sale. Once you can ensure they aren't talking themselves out of sales, then you can work on the prospects' thoughts.

Ultimately, just know that it's only their consideration or yours that is the barrier that is stopping the sale. Mind over matter is never truer than in sales.

Sales Is a Game of Intention

Sales is a game of intention. At Richter, we apply intention in everything we do, including selling. It's ranked above everything else, even technique. Intention will get the deal done even when technique is out. You have to intend for the prospect to buy. You have to believe in the product or service so firmly and know that it will help the client's company so completely that your confidence that the prospect will buy comes across on the phone or in person.

We sell from the viewpoint that we work for our clients' companies. In other words, it's as if we are internally working at their companies and we are strongly recommending that they get this product or service because we believe it will improve the company. We deliver the sales communication with that intention.

The *New Oxford American Dictionary* defines *intend* as:

to have (a course of action) as one's purpose or objective; plan
design or destine (someone or something) for a particular purpose or end

And *intention* is defined as:

a thing intended; an aim or plan

So, you must have intention for the prospect to buy. When you're hit with objections or considerations from the prospect, you can take them lightly, laugh them off, and say, "Joan, the reason I am pushing this a little is because I know it will work. I know what we do works, and once we get past the part where you're buying, you will too. I want you to buy and be a client of ours so we can help expand your company. I'm very confident in what we do, and I know we will have a huge impact on your sales. That's the reason and that's why I want you to get started today."

Care about prospects and their companies as if they were your own. Sell as if you are selling something you truly believe in and believe your clients need to invest in. Have intention and drive the sale to completion, with that intention channeled through all possible stops and barriers until the sale is done. People buy on intention, and it will outperform any technique, method, or smooth talking all day long. Intention comes from the gut and the heart, not the head. Sell with full intention, and your numbers will soar.

Considerations Bog Sales

If you have ever experienced a sale that seems to come to a slow halt and moves into waiting mode, it's likely due to a consideration that has not been handled by the sales rep. In other words, the prospect has a concern that your product or service won't handle the company's problem or has some other concern about it that he or she isn't telling you.

You need to find out what those concerns or considerations are so that you can address them. The second you can get the prospect to tell you what they are, you can then move to sell and close the deal, but up until that point, it's basically dead in the water.

Once handled, the cycle can go from something that was quickly becoming a future cycle or possibly a killed cycle, to one that happens now. It's a massive time-saver.

A great way to handle this is to e-mail the prospect and ask him or her point-blank, "Is there any consideration or concern you have that I haven't gone over that would prevent you from moving forward. Let me know so I can help." Then once you have gotten the feedback, handle it with whatever is needed: a case study, a client testimonial, a video that really sells the product, a phone call to walk the prospect through the process—whatever it may be that will handle the consideration. The point here is that you need to know what's stopping the person from moving forward first. From there you can handle it. But don't attempt to handle something when you don't know what it is that you're trying to handle.

Order Taker versus Salesperson

Sales is a funny game. In my opinion there are two kinds of people in sales: order takers and salespeople. An order taker is someone who waits for prospects to walk through the door, calls them, e-mails them, and then simply defines what they sell and handles the order for prospects as needed—that is, he or she essentially makes the sale only when prospects sell themselves. A salesperson is someone who actively works the deal; handles prospects' concerns, objections, and considerations; and makes the deal happen. A salesperson makes sales happen. An order taker simply facilitates a sale.

Being an order taker is easy. Being a salesperson is challenging; it takes discipline, skill, confidence, and control to make deals happen. Salespeople are rare. Order takers are abundant. Make a conscious choice to be a salesperson and then really decide in your own mind to become a *pro*. Study everything and work your deals to make them happen. Focus on the steps that need to be executed next and then go execute them. Write down the considerations, objections, or concerns; come up with a solution; and call the prospect to handle them. MAKE THINGS HAPPEN. Conclude deals and push cycles to a done status. Salespeople control cycles to cause the outcome they want, and they push each step forward until it's done. Don't use the word *wait*; that's for order takers.

If you want to win in sales, be a salesperson not an order taker.

Two Comments on Sales

Here are two points that are critical for sales:

1. *Fresh Lineup:* Always, always, always make a fresh lineup the night before. A lineup is composed of the active sales prospects you're working, including the associated revenue (the dollar amount), company name, prospect

name, and next steps needed to close the deal. Review your overall lineup for the week and then write in a notepad the prospects that you intend to close deals with the following day. When you get to work, you can simply open your notepad and begin. Don't do anything else outside of working that lineup to sell and close them. Once done, work the rest of your lineup for the week or handle new prospects. Even if you have a lineup for the entire week, you need a new fresh lineup for each and every day that details what deals will be closed that day, and it needs to be created the night before so you're prepared and ready for each day. This action alone will drive sales like crazy. Make it a habit.

2. *Hustle after Affluence:* Never get relaxed after an affluent week or day. When you have a big week or day, you need to throw things into high gear rather than becoming complacent. Stay hungry. You were successful because you worked your tail off the week or day prior. Keep that same level of action to make it happen again. If you let things slide, you hurt yourself and the group, so be committed and disciplined and avoid becoming lax. Push yourself to *always* beat your personal best. Never be content. Never be satisfied. Maintain this attitude, and you will really flourish.

Additional Sales Tips

A few points brought up at a sales meeting were so on point that I was compelled to write them down to study, know, and apply:

1. Don't spend too much time on small deals. If the deal isn't closing and the prospect seems to be dragging his or her feet, be as upfront or outspoken as you can. For example, call the prospect and say, "I can understand why you may be taking your time to decide on this, but I wanted to stress that this service may just be the element in your sales strategy that helps loosen things up to create some new income that allows you to expand. And this price is not going to cause the company any harm, so let's move forward on this." This is just an example, but the point is, hit them between the eyes and work to close the deal right there. Your time is valuable and can't be wasted on small deals that take a long time to close. Focus on being fast and to the point on the smaller ones; then work to close the larger deals.

2. Focus on the *next steps*. In other words, name the immediate next step in the sequence of actions to take for each deal. Don't just say, "Well, I need to call them or e-mail them." That's a given. We know that. But what do you need to *do*? What action will you take when you call the prospect? Does the prospect need a proposal? Do you need to handle his or her consideration about *x*? Focus on the next step, clearly name what it is, and execute it.

3. Be proactive and send a proposal to every prospect. Don't wait for a prospect to ask you for one. If you have an idea what level of service or product you need to sell to that company, proactively create the proposal and send it with an e-mail that reads, "John,

I sent a proposal for the [product or service], which is what I recommend we do. If you're ready to get started, simply sign it and send it back and we will get the process rolling. Thanks!" Every prospect in your pipeline needs to have a proposal. If they don't, get them one today.

How to Fill Your Day

Being in sales, you need to run yourself. In other words, you need to manage yourself. You need to be disciplined and keep yourself on track daily and push yourself to attain higher levels. A sales manager can help with this, but the truth is, the best salespeople run themselves hard and push themselves to hit new highs.

Here is a list of things you should be filling your day with in order to be productive and attain sales consistently:

Sending Follow-up E-mails: Review your sales lineup every day (not just hot prospects but all of your prospects) and send follow up e-mails. Make them smart. Make sure they communicate to prospects. Don't send some bland follow-up message. Do this daily.

Making Phone Calls: Call everyone on your sales lineup to work the deal forward. You are trying to push the deal to the next step in order to close it. Again, be smart. Figure out what to say. Call everyone you can think of. Review all prospects: hot, cold, warm—it doesn't matter. Just stay on the phone with people. Have conversations. You should spend 80 percent of your time on the phone. Figure out how to keep yourself on the phone. Do this, and you will have a lot of sales and be consistent.

Booking Appointments: If a prospect cannot speak now, book an appointment, set it on your calendar, and send the person a calendar invite. The more overall appointments you have, the more opportunities you will have to be on the phone to close sales.

Daily Planning: Either the night before or first thing in the morning, make a plan that names the targets for that day and clearly names the lineup for sales. Be prepared. A big part of sales is being organized and clearly naming the targets for the day. Make a clear plan and focus on executing it daily.

Prospecting: If you are not in the middle of an immediate cycle, spend time daily prospecting. Go online, find companies that may be a fit, and e-mail or call them. Or look through old prospects or past client lists and reach out to those you haven't spoken to in a while. Do this daily, and you will be inundated with business.

Learning about Your Prospects: Take some time to study up on the active prospects you are working. Go to their sites and see what they do. Then you can get a few ideas for what they need and what to sell to them.

Studying: Read sales books or sales material to get better at your craft. If you're not doing this, you'll be left behind in skill and competence. The best salespeople study all the time to learn everything they can to help refine what they do or remind them what works. You can never know it all, so don't pretend you do. Be smart and continue to read and educate yourself to get better at sales.

It's easy to get lazy in sales and wait for things to come to you or fall in your lap, but the truth is, sales happen because you make them happen. That's how it works. So nail these points, and you will have consistent numbers week in and week out. Remember, in sales, you can create whatever you want incomewise; the only barrier to attaining your goals is you.

Causative Sales

Through hard-won experience, we have found a few key operating bases for sales. Sales is a game, much like a sport, which means you have to play to win and play from a competitive advantage. As long as you are absolutely sold on what you are selling and you are sold on the idea that the prospect actually needs it and will benefit from it, then you can apply the following points aggressively to win more sales.

Here are the ways to apply speed and control to increase the number of deals closed:

1. *Never deal with "vias."* In other words, don't let a middle person on the sales cycle sell for you. Sometimes you are dealing with someone in the sale who is

not powerful enough to make a decision and must go to his or her senior, boss, or CEO. Don't let this occur. If you are selling to a via (middle person), control the cycle to set up a phone call or meeting where you attend when the via takes the proposal to his or her boss or the person responsible for making a decision. This will give you an opportunity to sell the deal right there, handle objections, and close the deal. If you allow the via to sell for you, there is a pretty good chance the deal will be lost. Don't sell through vias; sell with them to the decision maker to control the cycle and make sure it is clearly sold, duplicated, and closed. Selling through vias is sloppy.

2. *Never allow a multitopic meeting with your proposal to be "one" of the topics to discuss.* If the prospect says, "We are going to have a multitopic meeting to discuss the proposal and make a decision," divert the cycle to suggest an A-to-B phone call or meeting specifically about the proposal to save them time and you time by keeping everyone on the same topic and able to address the points and answer all of the questions, objections, and so on, in one call or meeting. This is a much more effective and desirable method. Justify this with the prospect by saying something along the lines of, "Meetings tend to deviate from the main goal when there are a lot of topics. And it's pretty common for questions to come up, which means we will need to meet or have a call anyway, adding time for both of us. We have found that it's best to simply have a call dedicated to the one topic of the proposal. That way

we can explain everything in a fraction of the time." The bottom line here is to stick to your internal sales flowchart and keep the deal on track and in your control.

3. *Never believe a prospect who says "next week."* There is *no* next week, ever. "Next week" is a procrastination move and stall tactic used by many prospects. In business, time is of the essence. Time is your enemy, and speed is your friend. Make the cycle urgent and control and steer the cycle to ensure that whatever needs to happen, it happens this week. Your goal is to make a good deal today because next week, or tomorrow for that matter, never comes. If a prospect suggests next week, ask what happens next week and then propose an idea like, "Tell you what, our CEO is in town this week, and I'd like to get him to weigh in on this cycle. Can we have a call first thing Thursday morning with you and anyone who needs to be on the call to answer any and all questions in one fell swoop?" Make the cycle urgent and put the control back in your court to get the cycle completed. This alone will close more deals simply by taking the time out of the cycle.

Figure out how to control your sales cycles and apply speed to get deals done, and I assure you the preceding three points will help you close more deals, faster.

On Operations

A Note on IKEA

I made a trip to IKEA with my family this past week and thought I would comment on their business model. To start, I feel everyone has something to learn from IKEA. Here are a few key points that can and should be applied to your company:

1. *Demonstration Sales Presentation:* If you have ever been to an IKEA store you know that the entire store is built as a full tour or live demonstration of their product offerings. It's basically Disney World for grown-ups looking for home furnishings and accessories. This is a smart approach to sales. Customers get to see the products and get a clear picture of what those products might look like in their homes. Arrows throughout the stores guide customers where the company wants them to go and point out what IKEA wants them to see, which results in control of the customer. By the time customers are done with the tour/demo, they should have seen and now know what they want and have added it to their carts. The tour/demo model is a phenomenal way to sell your product because it makes the product or service real to the potential buyer. Find a way to demo your product to your possible buyers in a way that allows them to compare it to how they will

actually use the product or service. This will help control and improve your sales.

2. *Fun:* The entire experience is fun. It doesn't feel like shopping or a chore. It feels like you are at a massive theme park for home furnishings and accessories. The vibrant colors and entire layout make it fun to walk through and look at products. Photos about the company's history, latest products, and so on, hang on the walls, making the entire experience incredible. Building in some fun will result in happy customers, which will result in buyers, which will result in income.

3. *Catering to Your Public:* A *huge* elevator in the middle of the store fits tons of people comfortably. A beautifully designed food court caters to hungry guests. The store layout is perfect to easily maneuver through. There is a child center to leave the little kiddos to play to their hearts' content while allowing the parents to casually stroll through the store. And for those who want to bring the tykes along, there are kid-friendly pockets and sections throughout the store. Helpful staff are spread all around. The checkout is a breeze. Need I say more? Everything in its design is set up to take good care of their customers and to make them happy so that they can enjoy their shopping experience and spend more money.

4. *Exchange:* The prices are unreal. IKEA is clearly providing value. I'm not by any means cheap or a bargain shopper, but I can appreciate value and love the idea of getting a great a bargain. IKEA has this pegged. The prices for the items and the overall

experience are well below the actual value, which makes IKEA's exchange with its customers through the roof. Figure out a way to provide a higher value to your clients than what they would pay for your product or service and you will always ensure long-term survival for your company. When I say value, I don't mean price. Value can be a lot of things that makes the customer feel they got more than what was paid for. If the prospect bought a sales training program for $1000 but it helped drive their sales by $100,000, in their mind, the value was well over what they paid for.

I am certain that there are more takeaways from IKEA than I have listed here, but these were the basics that I wanted to make notes on. Go and see for yourself. It clearly had an impact on me, which has created another obvious benefit that will build their sales: customer word of mouth. Kudos to you, IKEA.

Fast Decisions Make Time

It's pretty common to hear people complain about not having enough time or being too busy. There never seems to be enough time, right? Too much work and not enough time to do it. However, a huge part of the problem is not related to how much time there is; it's related to what people do to themselves that cause bottlenecks in their schedules and gobble up their time.

I could list many, many examples of this, but for the purpose of keeping this short and sweet, I will name just one: decisions. Or more specifically, taking forever to make them. Here's an example: Your company needs a product or service that has been discussed in the past, and everyone agrees that it's something you do, indeed, need or want. You have found a company to do the work and all seems to look good. At this point, rather than making an immediate decision to move forward swiftly to get what you want, meetings are held, e-mails are exchanged, time is added, approval is sought from the appropriate people, questions and objections are voiced . . . You know this example well, I'm sure.

If you observe this situation or any situation like it, you can clearly see where your time goes. It gets eaten up by what should be the simplest of things. Learn to make fast decisions and you will learn the art of creating time— *way* more time! Do not hesitate to pull the trigger on decisions. Make them fast and make them now. By disciplining yourself to get into this habit, you can get a lot more done. You will start to have an abundance of time. Time is not the issue; the issue is those things that waste time and gobble up the time you do have. Focus on making fast decisions for everything and on completing cycles related to decisions immediately, and you will start to recapture your time.

Excitement Fuels a Company

Tons of business books discuss ideas on management, sales, operations, and culture, among many other different concepts, but one key element that plays a critical role in growth for the company is being left out: excitement. It's a contagious feeling. If the company or what you are doing is exciting, it will catch fire with prospects and your people. They will start getting excited too, which leads to positive actions and growth for the company. It's a bit of an *x* factor in any successful formula for any company, and it isn't talked about a lot. For me, my company excites me. I get excited to come to work in the morning. I think about the various plans and goals or visions for the future that I have, and it excites me. When I am working on closing a deal with a large client, I get excited about the service we'll provide and about their company. I can visualize how we are going to help the client and what needs to happen. Simply by talking about it, I get excited. This excitement comes across on the phone and in person. The client can see it on my face and hear it in my voice. Then the client proceeds to get excited, and the next thing I know, we are closing the deal based on that excitement. It's actually hard to resist getting excited when you're around someone who is.

With my people, I get excited about our future and what they bring to the table; they, in turn, get excited, which gears them up to come up with better ways to do their job. Excitement reinvigorates people so that they start doing great work. Excitement is completely and utterly contagious and has a very positive effect on any company. Use it in sales to get your sales team excited and, in turn, get them to get their prospects excited. Use it when meeting with any of your staff to get them excited and, in turn, get them to produce or execute their jobs better. Use it with yourself to drive a forward thrust that will help fuel your company's ideas and growth. It's powerful stuff. No one likes being around boring, uninterested people. Excitement is part of the reason why people buy fast cars, travel to exotic places, and admire people like Richard Branson of Virgin or Steve Jobs of Apple, both of whom have created excitement within their companies.

People crave excitement. Figure out how to get yourself excited and how to make your product or service exciting and convey that excitement to your prospects, customers, and staff. It will help fuel everything about your company and solidify your growth. Hell, it's exciting just to type this section about excitement . . . it gets me thinking about what I want to talk about next. See, it's contagious!

Can I? Yes. Should I? No.

When you're a highly talented and able person, you tend to try to take on everything yourself. I get it. It's easier to just do it yourself than have someone else do it, right? As the saying goes, If you want something done right . . . But that's not a very productive motto to live by for a company. You have to learn to use your people and train them to be able to attain the exact result that you desire without having to worry about every detail yourself. Everyone has his or her place in a company. Similar to a baseball team, people have their exact roles. Sure, perhaps a great baseball player can play every position on the field, but it makes no sense to try to do so and is totally impractical. If that were the case, you wouldn't have a team.

Everyone in the company has his or her position, and you have to allow each employee to play it. In fact, you have to demand every employee play it. Empower your employees to play it and trust them to play it. It will take some training, drilling, and patience on your part, but the end result makes it worth the effort. Once you get a full team up and running doing the work, it's a dream team. I have a phrase that goes through my head every time there's a chance for me to leave my position and take on someone else's position: "Can I? Yes. Should I? No." Then, once fully decided that I shouldn't take over someone else's position, I delegate the task to the right person and provide correction if problems arise or that person can't do it.

I also send employees to training if they are having problems that are getting in the way of doing their job because it means that they don't know something about their position. First, I give them the task and expect and trust them to do it. I don't do it for them or answer questions about it to help them do it. I just assign it to them and let them know that they are in charge of it. You would be amazed at how many people will rise to the occasion and get the result you want—or one very close. The trend seems to be to bypass people and do their work for them. This needs to stop. It will only breed incompetence. When you do try to assign work to people who have been treated this way, they may not know how to do a task or numerous problems may occur when they try. But if you handle these situations correctly, they will gain skills and confidence and they will step up to the task to get it done. People are natively pretty smart and capable; it's just that, over the years, they have had that nullified and therefore think less of their abilities.

When you challenge people and empower them to step up to the plate and trust them to, they will. It takes only a few times of this pattern before people are competently doing their jobs without any handholding. Focus on pushing power to your people. Train them, delegate to them, and allow them to take responsibility and accountability for tasks and then trust them to do it and let them. You'll be amazed at how much comes off your plate and how much more time and energy you will have to do your job. You do have your own duties, so don't forget that when you are taken off your position, no one is covering it, which means your position suffers because you are not allowing your people to handle theirs. Organize, train, and build a true team similar to a professional baseball team; allow and expect everyone to cover his or her positions—it's a game changer. And if one or two people simply can't maintain their positions competently no matter how many tools you've given them to do so, you'll be able to see that for what it is and make decisions accordingly.

Time Is Not Your Friend, But Speed Is an Ally

Many people, while acting busy and seeming as if they are frantically producing, are quite wasteful of time. It doesn't take that much time to accomplish most tasks, but time is most definitely not your friend. It relentlessly ticks forward. It will never stop to give you a minute to catch up. That's the way it is. It's important to understand that. Once you have a clear grasp of how time actually works, you can then work to use it to your advantage. The way to take charge of time is to understand speed and its role in creating forward motion that will drive your actions and company to create a sort of inertia. You need to be able to clearly list the various actions or targets related to an overall game plan that you can then apply speed to. In other words, the clearer you can list accurate targets that attain your goals and the faster you can execute actions one by one, the more you will start to understand how speed helps you.

The slower you go, the more you will understand how time works against you. The same is true if your targets (or goals) are foggy or so generalized that it prevents them from being easily executed. If the target is not broken down to its simplest format, like "pick up the phone and call Tom Johnson at 3PM today" but instead it's "call prospects today to close sales" the sales rep goes slow because he or she has a hard time getting going on the first action. Think swiftly and work out simple, doable targets and then execute them as fast as possible, focusing on only one target at a time until it is done. There's a lot of hubbub out there about multitasking, but it's actually very counterproductive. Focus on one target and execute it swiftly. Get your entire company to pick up the pace. You will be amazed at what can be accomplished if you inject speed into the organization. Speed leaves no time to think things over, which means you need to act on instincts and you need to make fast decisions. By forcing immediate actions and immediate decisions, you will also remove any and all indecisions that slow down progress and gobble up valuable time. The funny thing about making decisions is that even when you take the time to "think it over," it doesn't result in a better decision. You could have made the same decision in 20 seconds rather than in 4 weeks. The only difference in the decisions is that you wasted 4 weeks that could have been spent on many other things, not to mention the fact that it gobbles up your attention. So focus on forcing speed into play, and by doing so you will see that you will be forced to make instant decisions and then take instant actions to execute those decisions. At that point you will experience the magic of speed and once and for all show time who's in charge.

Basic Operating Basis Rules

We have developed a few basic operating bases at our agency that I have given to our management team to use daily in their efforts to attain our goals. It's easy to get distracted by the noise from all areas in a company but as a manager, you simply need to focus your time and energy on a few key points. Here they are:

- Get people working. Get people in their chairs producing their respective products. Don't let people wander around or cause confusion. Route them to their desks and get them to get their work done.

- Give orders. Come in each day and create orders as needed for your area and assign them to your people; then follow up to ensure you get compliance. See each order through until it's done.

- Make rapid decisions and take action. Do not delay decisions and "think" about them. Make immediate decisions and put those decisions into action immediately. Time is not your friend, but speed is an ally. Any decision that needs to be made, make it on the spot, assuming you have enough information. If you don't have enough information, round up what's needed immediately and make the decision. Then focus all attention to move the decision into action right away. Speed will help you get to affluence, so focus on consistent forward motion.

- If there is something to do, do it now. Get your battle plan knocked out immediately, one cycle after the next. Do not waste time because there isn't any time to waste.

Getting into Communication

Over and over, I notice many people and companies are out of communication or at least have lethargic communication systems. What I mean by that is they are slow to the draw, slow to reply, slow to take action, or don't take any action at all.

Communication is the very essence of business as well as the economy. The more you can create and the faster you can get it going, the more revenue flows. In fact, if you had to name one critical factor as more important to your success than any other, you could name the speed of your communication as ranking above all others.

Currently it seems there is quite a problem with communication. As a business owner myself, I value the importance of communication above all else. I demand from my staff that a lot of communication goes out to the world, more specifically, to our target audience. I also demand that we handle communication rapidly, as fast as we can, to keep our flows moving fast.

If I receive an e-mail from someone interested in our company, we instantly reply to move the cycle forward. Phone calls are returned the same day, and everyone in the company has a mobile device that allows for immediate response via e-mail at any given time. In addition, we developed the Social Media Press Kit (http://whywebpr.com) to make ourselves more accessible in every imaginable way, be it text message, e-mail, Skype, Facebook, or LinkedIn, or to download our communication details through a vCard.

We rate communication highly. However, I have noticed that not everyone operates this way. People delay in responding via e-mail or phone. They are slow to communicate many times, if at all. This type of operating basis hurts them and their company. Procrastination has no place in the business world. Slowness is not a strength, and being out of communication is damaging. The way to handle it is each item is a separate task and to answer communication as it comes in but not to interrupt the immediate task you are on but rather, handle it next. The main point is to be a swift as possible with all communication. Multitasking is a massive distraction and not at all advised at any company.

Take a look at your communication systems this week and test them. Do you immediately respond to e-mails? Phone calls? How much communication are you sending out to the world daily? Is that enough?

If handled properly, your revenue will skyrocket. Get yourself and your company into the habit of communicating with the world. Send communication out, even if you simply start by sending out 6 handwritten letters per week or 10 e-mails to introduce yourself to people you want to do business with. Get communication flowing and moving quickly.

And by the way, communication doesn't mean simply shouting into the wind. A communication means actually identifying your audience and then communicating something that they find relevant to their needs—and doing it in a way that actually gets their attention and captures their interest.

Part of the reason people hate spam so much is that it's so painfully obvious that the message is not directed to them or their needs. We strive to be the polar opposite of spammers, making every communication as direct, relevant, and personalized as we possibly can. We value the time of our prospects, clients, and associates, and we work to remind them of that with every communication.

Getting Organized

I want to make a brief comment about the importance of being organized and having clear systems and administration for your company: I personally believe that a huge amount of profit is lost in this area. A lot of companies are strong in sales, delivery, or customer service, but not many are truly strong in administration, that is, in process, operations, systems, and so on. Think it through and make a checklist of the areas that need to be addressed.

Here is a starting point:

- Flowcharts for all key areas and functions, such as sales, delivery, and finance, posted on the wall so that they are viewable for training and drilling
- Progress boards to monitor and track key actions so that you can manage and push progress week to week
- Clearly defined positions and actions for each person in written format so that your people can study them and become competent at their positions
- A form of measurement for all key company indicators that can be tracked weekly to compare week to week and to set targets for improvement
- Checklists or procedures for handling specific actions such as collecting income, closing sales, and delivering to new clients in order to have exact sequences that are followed every time, without fail

These are just a few basic fundamental points to look into. The message here is that, time and time again, I see companies lose opportunities and income simply through lack of planning, lack of systems, and lack of organization, which result in chaos and confusion in the company, making people look busy when, in fact, it's totally unproductive motion.

By clearly defining all systems and functions and ensuring all procedures are organized in all areas, your production level will go through the roof. It's not time you lack; it's a lack of administration that organizes processes to create more time for you. Inefficiencies are expensive and a drain financially and logistically. Define the sequence of events that everything needs to go through within the company for each area. For example, we have a flowchart that defines our sales process from start to finish that the sales team follows to understand what the next steps are and so they just follow the process. Otherwise, everyone does things a little differently and it can become very inefficient as people attempt to invent systems for you.

Our agency tends to get about a month's worth of work done in a week simply because we are organized and can execute and have systems for everything. Don't run around and say you're busy and have no time. Get organized, be ruthless about your systems, and create time for yourself in order to focus on doing more to expand your company. Dissect your processes and jam in orderly operations, and you'll see what I mean.

Introductions

Defining the parameters of the platforms you use to establish and maintain your relationships online is vital to making your products and services known to the correct public. Consider the total time, money, and energy you put into marketing your business. Are you satisfied with your results? Are you reaching those people most likely to be interested in your products and services without feeling the need to carpet bomb the entire World Wide Web?

"Work smarter, not harder" is especially applicable in the social media universe. Connecting to any random person on social media, sending out mass marketing–style e-mails, and blasting blogs constantly, but never taking the time to really introduce yourself to the correct audience, is definitely working hard, not smart. Social media is full of people waiting to be found. In fact, never in history have so many people been so willing to share their contact information and the vital details of the kind of work they do so freely. It's a gold mine of free and usually accurate information.

Take the time to find the appropriate person and introduce yourself. You may not have a network of 23,000 friends and fans in the next six weeks, but what would that actually accomplish in terms of gaining new business anyway?

Building relationships with the correct public for your company can be easy once you make a sincere introduction. A great rule to live by is to send out only the exact kind of message you yourself would like to receive as a busy professional. Start simply, with basic information about who you are and what you do, and find out what might be needed or wanted from you by the person receiving the message. And don't forget to invite the recipient to respond in kind, and when he or she does, really listen and acknowledge what that person is communicating in return.

Selling your services and products to someone you've taken the time to forge a genuine connection with brings in more business, and it's more enjoyable to both parties. Leave the spam to spammers. Life and business are about people. Always remember there's another "you" on the receiving end of every communication, and you'll see great results from all that social media has to offer.

Speed

Have you ever truly looked over the value of speed as it relates to your company's growth, strategies, sales, delivery, and expansion? I personally rate this as one of the highest-valued items in our agency and in any company.

Speed is how fast you can move an idea into execution to make that idea a reality. Speed is your friend, and time is your enemy. Speed of delivery is how fast you can deliver your product or service with the highest level of quality. Speed of sales is how fast you can find your audience, prospect, sell, and close a deal to create hoards of new business.

Speed is something you should measure, if you don't already. People talk frequently about competition, what the other companies are doing, and so on. If you master speed, the truth is, there isn't any real competition out there. Most companies are slow. Most people are slow.

Competition is a highly overrated concept. Focus on speed, and the "competition" becomes something that you view from a distance in your rearview mirror while you scratch your head, wondering how and why they don't get it.

Even looking at today's economy, if people and companies operated faster, new companies started faster, decisions were made faster, and speed became a central and crucial element of the marketplace, we wouldn't have a problem. The economy would recover swiftly, and new fresh funds would be produced and circulated quickly.

Sometimes simple answers are the hardest to figure out, but they ultimately prove to be the best solutions.

Make a point this week and next to execute tasks faster. Speed up your cycles. Look for ways to take time out of the equation to increase your production. Look at all the applications of speed and figure out how to put them into action.

- Speed of sales
- Speed of promotional ideas to get them into action
- Speed of quality delivery
- Speed of internal communications
- Speed of external communications
- Speed of news to the market
- Speed of promotional updates or changes such as websites
- Speed of hiring and training
- Speed of executing actions
- Speed of meetings and phone calls

Although this may sound a little overboard, it's not, I assure you. There is slowness all throughout your personal actions day to day as well as throughout your company, and I promise, it's costing you the game. Take speed seriously. Get disciplined about it and your "competition" will become a silly concept. Companies are slow, people are slow . . . take advantage of it.

Client Prediction

As it relates to clients and servicing them, client prediction is a vital element to delivery and keeping clients happy and winning.

If there is ever any doubt in your mind about how your team is delivering or servicing your clients and whether the client is happy, handle it immediately, swiftly, and proactively. *Do not* wait for a client to speak up or originate communication to you or your team.

What is meant by prediction is this: if you sense in any way that the client is out of communication with you or your team or that a possible problem could occur or if any nonoptimal situation is perceived in *any* regard by you, handle it *immediately*.

By *handle*, I mean write down what you think might be wrong—what might be brewing—and then address it immediately. In addition to that, start live communication (i.e., via the phone) with the client and let your contact know that you are doing A, B, and C right now. This lets your contact know that you are working to address the immediate concerns. Then, while on the phone with the client, ask if there is anything specific he or she needs or wants in addition to what you just mentioned.

The concept here is to predict outcomes, confront them immediately, handle them, and keep the client happy and in good communication with you.

On Focus

Successful Principles

Over the years we have developed a few core principles that have resulted in a lot of success for our agency. Here they are, in no particular order of importance:

1. *Revenue, Not Budgets:* Budget meetings and budgetary concerns can easily distract an entire executive team and alter priorities. Business owners forget that budgets are created by driving revenue. Without revenue, it's pointless to repeatedly assess the budget. The focus must shift fully to actions that will drive revenue in order to generate fresh income that can cover and exceed budgets. It's not possible to cut expenses to attain affluence, so companies must zero in on every item within their company that can be a profit center and then take methodical actions to make it so.

2. *Weekly Measurements:* Quarterly numbers are important to keep but not the best method to help you keep your finger on the pulse of the business and better ensure survival. Measure all key numbers weekly and keep a graph that shows what each statistic, such as income or number of sales, is doing from week to week. Measuring weekly and managing weekly can help you avoid a catastrophe that would be hard to handle or correct if you were measuring only quarterly.

Know every vital number, measure and act on them weekly, and take every action to correct and push all numbers by the week.

3. *Survey to Clarify Needs:* Survey your clients or prospective clients monthly to focus your efforts on what they need or want, which will give insight into what should be marketed and sold. We use short surveys created on Google Doc forms that consist of only five to seven questions. The surveys can be e-mailed as a link each month. Each survey should be topic- or theme-specific as well. For example, if you're trying to figure out what made the client buy your product or service, align the survey questions to expose those specific answers. Don't make survey questions that are "yes" or "no" answers; create questions that encourage feedback so that you can use the data to improve operations and deliver what your clients revealed they need or want. Then tally all of the survey results to find the common denominators that show up in the results and incorporate those results into your marketing, sales, and delivery areas. By identifying key pain points, you ensure sales will expand and avoid wasting time on expensive marketing and sales campaigns that are not hitting the mark with your audience. If you take the time to find out exactly what your customers will buy and then ensure you are delivering those items, it will result in a less resistive path to revenue.

4. *Training:* Write what each person in the company is ideally supposed to do and create a training book for

each position. Take the best person or most experienced person in each area and extrapolate his or her successful actions, detailing all the ins and outs of the position. You will want to have a thorough write-up explaining all aspects of the job for all key positions. Then create a training pack from that material that includes a checklist detailing the sequence of how to study the training pack. Run your people through the training pack that applies to their position, such as sales reps or production director, until they have studied all of the material. This one thing has resulted in competent and productive staff for our agency. This will also dramatically reduce the time it takes to get a new hire up to speed and producing for your company. There are external training courses you can send your people through, but the best knowledge that should be used for training is right within your organization. Focus on the simple, doable actions that make up a particular job's daily routine and write them out in sequence. You'll be amazed at how breaking things down into their simplest elements takes the time out of getting new hires up and running, and it allows you to really examine the workflow and tasks assigned to each person.

5. *Focused Target Public:* Know your public. Take a look at who have been the most successful customers for your company and profile them to identify the common denominators. Then create a defined profile for who your ideal target public really is. Focus all sales and marketing efforts on only companies and people

who fit the audience you defined in the profile. This one strategy will dramatically drive growth because you're directing your efforts to the people most likely to do business with you.

Identifying the Common Denominators

It's amazing how many companies, large and small, don't know who their target public is. They think they know but generally they don't. They may rattle off generalized demographic information but generally have not completely nailed it down. In fact, many companies believe their target public is a broad spectrum or anyone and everyone. It's a lazy approach that ultimately requires huge sums of effort—it's difficult to sell to anyone and everyone. I can tell you from experience that I have never come across one company that sells to everyone and anyone or just the broad public. It doesn't exist. This can be easily proved by simply dissecting and profiling a company's current client lists and finding the common denominators associated with them. It's a revealing exercise and one that we find results in an epiphany for most of our clients. Once you can completely identify your audience and zero in on your ideal candidate, you then have a clear profile to whom you can promote, market, survey, and sell.

Many talk about low-hanging fruit but few actually identify every aspect of what the fruit looks like, feels like, smells like, where it hangs from, what color it is, as well as any other related specifics that would help create a visual profile of exactly what to look for. By doing that, you can spend your time wisely and efficiently drive new business with those most likely to buy from you. Every product or service has a buyer; most just don't know it or take the time to find out who that buyer is. When this is done correctly, you will have a clear picture of who buys from you, which means you won't need to worry about chasing everyone else. You can focus all of your marketing and sales efforts on only the people and companies most likely to buy from you. A simple and somewhat silly analogy would be if you sold pants and went downtown to a very busy street with many people walking toward you. Out of the crowd, there was one person not wearing any pants. If logic serves, it would make a heck of a lot of sense to go up to that person and try to sell him your pants, right? This is a simplistic example of what I mean but you get the general idea. Don't search for everyone and don't try to sell to the crowd. Sell to the guy who needs the pants. And if you really did your homework, you would have known that he was going to be walking down the street that day at that time in that city without any pants on. You would have had him nailed before he ever showed up, and you would have been waiting for him with everything you needed to sell him the pants: measuring tape, several pairs of pants, a credit card machine . . . you name it. You would have had your target public clearly identified and would have been prepared to sell him pants at the exact moment he needed them. It doesn't have to be so difficult to drive new business; you just need to know what you are looking for and where.

Goal Attainment

It's easy to get caught up in looking off into the distant future and at the overall goal of what you are trying to attain, but the actual way to attain your goal is by breaking it down into a series of small subgoals that, accomplished in an orderly sequence, ultimately attain the overall goal.

Many people have trouble with this and get beat up trying to attain a goal that never seems to come to fruition. Here is how to attain a goal:

1. Write down the overall vision that you want to attain. Make it crystal clear to ensure the goal is clearly defined.
2. Work out the sequence of actions that would likely be needed to attain the goal. In other words, list what you need to do specifically to attain it. List every possible step or action related to attaining the goal.
3. Take the first step or action and break it down into executable, doable targets.
4. Execute the first step and each individual target related to it.

Repeat steps 1 to 4 with the rest of your goal targets. Establishing goals and then planning how to attain each one, step by step, is vitally important. There's an old saying, "If you can't explain something to another person then you don't understand it yourself." Similarly, if you can't break down even the loftiest goal into individual, actionable steps, then you don't actually understand how to get there. On the other hand, once you have broken it down in this way, simply focus on executing the small subgoals within the overall goal and watch how things come together.

As an example, I run a lot and I have an overall goal that I'm trying to achieve. But I focus on the subgoals and then smaller subgoals within those subgoals. I get up every day and go for a run with a goal in mind, but even while running, I am focused only on the next step in front of me. I am looking to accomplish one concrete block step after the other concrete block step. I don't stare at the distance that I am running toward. I don't think about the overall fitness goal either. I win goal after goal, which are the small steps right in front of me; by focusing on those, I attain the overall distance goal for that day. Completing this one subgoal aligns with the overall goal of a fitness target.

Does that make sense? It's the breaking down of a goal into bite-sized chunks that are doable, executable targets that, put together, result in goal attainment. Work out the goal. Work out the planning. Work out the subgoals. Work out the subgoal targets. Execute daily.

Learn to Hate Butterflies

This may sound like a funny title, but the truth is butterflies are a serious problem in the business world—chasing them, that is. In today's busy and sometimes chaotic world it's easy to get distracted and end up dreaming or chasing butterflies rather than staying the course and focusing on your goals, your mission, and the immediate tasks at hand. My advice: learn to hate butterflies as well.

Focus on who you are, what you do, what the current and next goals are, and what the immediate step toward your goal is. Get focused on every aspect of your company:

- Know what target audience or vertical market you want to go after and exactly what you sell and what your value proposition is.
- Make sure that you aren't trying to be all things to all people.
- Get your people focused on their mission and tasks to attain your focused goal.
- Promote and sell to only your focused market.

There are innumerable things that can take you off course. Learn to spot them for exactly what they are: distractions, butterflies. Get rid of them and learn to simplify your company. Get focused and then get tunnel vision about that focus to work toward goal attainment. It may sound more fun or sexier to chase the constant new adventure or idea, but it's wasted time and effort. Chasing it prevents you from true victory and long-term goal attainment, which is the only way empires are built.

Take a look at any supersuccessful company or person, and you will see a very clear trend of the same thing being done with consistent improvement over time. A major reason for that kind of success is because the company or person was disciplined and stayed focused on the mission and goal.

Stop bouncing around and chasing possible ideas, the next new trend, or the latest fad and get focused on what you do or love and then work like mad on simplifying and making every facet of your company focused on that one goal and mission. There are countless examples that prove this to be the most workable method to success; conversely, there are countless examples that show that chasing butterflies is a surefire way to get you permanently lost in the woods.

Look

The value of thinking is grossly overrated. It's easy to get caught up in "thinking" through problems in business, but the value and application are limited. You need to look. Inspect and observe facts, statistics, and operations. Observe what is happening and how, and then collect applicable information that you can use and do something about. Look at how your sales reps are acting and speaking on the phone. Look at how your statistics charts are trending week to week and month to month. Look at how your delivery or production team is actually completing their tasks at hand. Simply stand by and observe while they work. Then based on things you actually see for yourself, make notes on items that need to be corrected and improved. By doing this, you will spot problems, bugged areas (problem areas within the company or related to people that need to be corrected), and nonoptimal operations. Now, with this factual and directly observable information in hand, you can act on it and create workable solutions not based on hunches but on real-world facts.

Stop trying to think your way through problems in order to arrive at a solution, because I promise, you will never arrive. You need to simply look and practice spotting the problems through intelligent observation. Then apply what you have learned to address the problem with practical solutions. Walk around and look daily at every area of the company to observe, take notes, and correct.

Anytime you start "thinking," switch over to looking and observing. You will find that the solution will flush out every time. This may sound overly simplistic, but it's more challenging than it might at first seem. However, you'll find it the fastest, simplest, and sanest way to make noticeable improvements in every area of your business. Plus, it's interesting and keeps you grounded and in touch with every aspect of your business, forcing you to confront situations and people who are not performing as well as they should and keeping you in control of the enterprise you are working so hard to build.

Work Ethic (Hustle)

A brief comment on work ethic: I try to challenge myself daily to work harder, get more done, be more disciplined, and push through more tasks or goals than the day before.

I have observed that by doing this, my level of action and discipline relative to that of most people is much higher. It's almost like working out in the gym to physically expand your limits and therefore increase the amount of weight you can carry or how many miles you can run daily. You may start out running half a mile, but if you push yourself daily, in a few months you can run 3 to 4 miles at a time.

Today's society is too lax about work, and its self-imposed limitations in terms of how hard it is willing to push is tiny. Don't allow yourself to fall into this category.

Challenge yourself to increase your work ethic. Push yourself, and you'll be amazed at what you are capable of.

- Make a daily agenda—tasks or actions that you must complete—and push them all through with zero reasonableness.
- Spend less time at lunch and wasting time daily so that you can execute your tasks at hand.
- Be disciplined about reading something productive daily to increase your knowledge.
- Engage in some kind of physical exercise daily to stay sharp and in good health. Don't smoke, take drugs, or drink to excess. This is not a moral imperative, but a factual one.
- When you think that you have completed your tasks, push a little harder to complete another few.

If you truly master your own work ethic, you will guarantee your survival and success. Push yourself and you will be an absolute asset no matter where you work.

Think of any sports team or event. Winners have an unbelievable work ethic. This is the one factor that is a constant with any winner. Don't allow yourself to simply be involved in the game; decide to win and then push yourself to grow into the type of person who has an incredibly high work ethic and who plays to win. Do this and you will find yourself winning as a matter of course.

I will warn you that it's actually very difficult to pull this off, and very few people who read this will actually do it. That is part of the reason that winners win. There are, frankly, very few people to compete with. Most people are lazy. Decide against being lazy and step up your entire game so that you can attain and have anything you want. The game of winning in life is actually very easy—you just have to be willing to work your tail off!

Do It Now

Nike said it best: "Just Do It"—except they left out the word "NOW." This is critical. Everything should be absolutely urgent to you. It must be done NOW. Take up each action one by one and handle them right now. No delays. I constantly force myself to be disciplined to apply this principle, and I can tell you with complete certainty that when I do this, we make progress like you wouldn't believe. When I don't, the whole day seems to slip out of my reach. I get bogged down by cycles that hit me from every angle. But if I handle my tasks now and execute relentlessly one by one, we make incredible progress. If someone interrupts you, let that person know you are in the middle of an action and you will handle his or her situation accordingly. Then write down what's needed in your tasks or have the person e-mail you the details. Then simply inject it into the order of targets or tasks that need to get done. But *do not* allow this interruption to distract you. Focus on what you are doing right now and get it done. Then handle the next target. Whatever it is that needs to be done, do it now. I could go into depth explaining why this works but I'm not going to—I want you to practice this and see for yourself. Tomorrow, make a list of what needs to be done for the day and practice applying this by doing each action now, one by one. Do not get distracted. Stay focused until each is done and then see where you end up at the end of the day. I already know how it's going to work out for you. Go do it now and you'll soon see what I mean.

All Things to All People

The thought of being all things to all people consistently mystifies me. I see agencies that are clearly traditional public relations (PR) houses and have extensive expertise in traditional PR and media that add things such as social media, new media, and search engine optimization to their service offerings. I also hear these same agencies tell their prospective clients, "Oh, yeah, we handle that, too" or "Yes, we can take care of the social." My first question is, What is "the social"? Please define.

In my experience the only people and companies that I have seen do extremely well are niche providers. I have yet to see watered-down companies do well at everything. Michael Jordan is an incredible basketball player. But baseball? Soccer? Not so much.

Companies that focus on what they are good at and what they know inside out do very well and are truly the companies to deal with for a specific need. If I have a need or a want regarding men's suits, it's a certainty that I will get better knowledge, customer service, and recommendations from a niche fine men's suit store than I will at Macy's. Although Macy's is a good store and has a wide variety, you won't find the very best in men's suits or in expertise regarding men's suits.

If you need a litigation attorney, go get a litigation attorney and don't try to get a general law firm that possibly can handle your litigation needs (and since you are hiring them anyway, maybe they can also do your legal papers and corporate filings and on and on). This strategy will lead to mediocre results. If that's what you are searching for, you can find that by the hoards. However, if you want the very best solution for your exact need or problem, my suggestion is to go with the niche, specialized people or companies. It's a smart move all around.

You wouldn't put all of your human resources (HR) work and recruitment work on your treasury or administrative people because they are somehow related, would you?

I would much rather be surrounded by niche specialists and companies that do incredible work and get the desired outcome I am going after because they know their stuff than have to try to find the one company that is trying to be everything to everyone, jamming every service under one roof and trying to make it all fit rather than truly focusing on what it is good at.

What Does It Take?

Have you ever really looked at what it takes to attain a goal? It's easy to make a goal and then work toward it, but that's really only half the exercise. You need to break it down. What are the component parts of the goal, and what are all of the steps needed to attain it?

Once you start working out the actual steps and any specific numbers or actions associated with attaining the goal, beef up your numbers because I can assure you that your numbers will be low in terms of estimation. People are masters at underestimating what is needed to attain a goal. You need to do your homework upfront, determine the actions necessary, and work out the correct effort needed to attain the goal. If you think you have overestimated it, that's okay because it means you're either right on track or you may produce slightly more, which is a plus point.

For your next project or goal, take some time to plan what it requires to make it happen. Don't just write down the plan or goal and then start pursuing it. Work out all of the actions that will be needed to pull it off. This will help shift your reality and open your eyes to the work involved to make it happen. As an example, if you were putting together a premade bookshelf and decided to write out your building plan, you wouldn't write, "Build it." Your plan would include things such as "Read instructions" and "Gather tools." You need to assess your sales goals the same way. What are the "instruction steps" associated with your goal? You can then better plan, predict, and execute the actions needed, which will make the target infinitely easier to attain and the overall probability of attainment skyrocket.

Be Focused to Drive Statistics

It's absolutely critical that you focus your time and energy on your exact position, duties, and tasks for each day. Do not get distracted by the random noise outside of your role. Remind yourself what your job is, what your position entails, and what you should be doing with your time.

Focus on completing targets and getting through your targets one step at a time each day. Do not engage in random chatter around the office or in discussions that have nothing to do with your position or area. Focus on what you need to do and do it.

If everyone is completely dialed in to the tasks at hand and focused and intent on getting the job done and making sure all the key targets are attained for their areas, the company will flourish. Everyone in the company needs to be able to count on coworkers being focused and getting their jobs done. When an entire company operates this way, it becomes a production machine that has a certain level of inertia that seems unstoppable. Companies excel as a group to the degree that they are focused daily on their duties and the tasks to get done for that day.

Be disciplined and stay focused. Cut out any possible distractions that arise. If someone interrupts you, let him or her know that you're in the middle of a task and need to focus on it. Trust me, others will understand and it then becomes the new operating basis for the company. Not many companies operate this way, but if you do, you'll be far ahead of the others.

On Marketing

A Lesson from Red Bull

When it comes to promotions and getting the word out, there is a standard by which you can measure yourself; it's called Red Bull. This is a company that thinks BIG. They have plastered their brand, public relations (PR), marketing, and advertising absolutely everywhere.

I guarantee you that if it were not for their unbelievably *huge* promotional efforts, the company would not be what it is today (which happens to be a billion-dollar annual revenue–producing machine). I don't find the drink exactly tasty, but that factor has no role in their success.

I admire this company for their sheer volume of promotions and in their creativity in getting the word out.

So, what can we learn? When looking at your promotional efforts, address volume and angles of approach. In other words, what are you doing right now? How much promotion and outflow—any and all communication being sent from your company out into the marketplace to prospective clients or to current clients—are you doing? How many avenues are you using daily, weekly, and monthly to make your company's products or services known? I think most companies grossly underestimate what they need to do. Companies get so focused on other things—things that are important but not nearly as important as bringing in new business.

Revenue should never be your concern. New clients should never be your concern. These things will come in floods if your promotion and sales efforts are sufficient—and not just sufficient per your "normal" standard; you need Red Bull–type thinking.

Make a list and focus on how you can create a Red Bull–sized strategy to get the word out. Get absolutely crazy about promotion and bringing in new business. And you don't need a Red Bull–sized marketing budget to make it happen. In the age of social and new media, there are more ways than ever to creatively connect with your target demographic. Most of the most popular videos on You-Tube, the world's second largest search engine, were made with no budget whatsoever. With your strategy in place, focus on executing that strategy in an obsessive fashion to bring new customers/clients in the door. From there, you can then figure out how to deliver, provide service, maintain quality, and so forth. But all of these items come after you have promoted, made your company known, and gotten new sales, clients, and customers. Your first priority should be on your front lines—promotion!

When you're scratching your head wondering why sales and revenue are down, look no further than your efforts to get the word out about your company and to actively get in front of your audience, thereby cultivating new opportunities. That is the *why*. Very simply put, the more you put your message out there, the more response you will see, period.

So this week, think like Red Bull—a company that has gone completely berserk when it comes to promotions and it's working like crazy. Make a list of new angles to drive in new business and execute, execute, execute.

Proactive versus Reactive

We started Richter to handle the very problem related to PR, advertising, and marketing companies' approach: they are reactive. Traditional methods create a campaign targeted to an audience and then get responses. From there, those responses can be filtered to trickle down to the buyers. For example, an advertising agency creates an ad and gets it out into magazines and online ads, etc., they attempt to target as best as possible via the magazine type and demographics as well as the website type and traffic demographic and then they get clicks and some responses like phone calls or e-mails and from there they need to qualify those responses to see if this is even the correct audience for the company to sell to and then some sales are made. Statistics show that this number is 1 to 2 percent. It's a reactive method, and it's old. We're proactive. We do our homework upfront to zero in on the exact public we want to target before we do anything. Once we know our audience, we seek them out, make an introduction, and develop the relationship from there to sell them a product or service. We don't need to trickle down or qualify the audience because we did it before we ever started.

Companies spend massive sums of money on traditional PR, marketing, and advertising, which gets results, sure, but not results like it should. We've gotten soft. We accept a 2 percent response rate. We're reasonable about it, and we really shouldn't be. You need to start looking at your marketing efforts in a proactive way and then push the response up over 50 percent. It can be done. We do it every day.

Right now, think about where your target public is. What tools do they use to communicate? How can you proactively reach them?

If you're spending money on things like online ads or keywords, take a good hard look and dig in to see if your audience or ideal clientele even pays attention to those types of things. You may find out that they never use the keywords you're paying for in their online searches or that they simply don't search at all. In other words, you need to search for them, rather than forcing them to search for you.

Somehow over the years we've forgotten about how human beings truly operate, and we've attempted to make prospects come to us in an automated structured way that hopefully will allow you to be as lazy as possible. An example of this is if a car dealer simply focused on campaigns that drove people through the front door of the dealership. That sounds nice, but what if people are trickling in like they are in today's economy? The dealer needs to know how to hunt for and reach out to the prospect in a proactive method. When prospects walk through the front door, they should treat it as a cherry on top but not as the core source of new prospects. What if the dealer discovered the number one trade-in for the brand it sells and then found every person in its geographic location who fit that profile. What if the dealer actually went out and found those people and made a short but personal introduction and gave them a card. Statistically, the people they are reaching out to are already most likely to be interested based on common denominators. So the dealer knows it is dealing with the right people and now simply needs to establish communication, relations, and interest to create a highly probable sale. A specific prospect may not have been thinking about buying a car right then, but the dealer effectively planted a seed in the mind of exactly the right person based on his or her profile. And that person is now thinking about buying a car . . . and interest comes up to a point of reach. Now the right person based on the criteria for that company in terms of an ideal customer is reaching toward a sale. They are strongly interested and are communicating something like "I'd like to come in and have a meeting with you" which we refer to as "reaching" or a "reach."

You should be dissecting all of your marketing, PR, and advertising campaigns and assessing whether what you're doing is proactive or reactive. If it's reactive, you're losing money.

Speaking Human

I can never fully understand why companies write copy for their websites or material that sounds so complex. People simply don't talk that way. Think about any casual setting where you've had a conversation with someone and business has come up in the conversation. How did it go? What was said?

Be authentic when writing copy. Be natural and communicate in human terms. Otherwise, you risk scaring people away or at least boring them half to death. People want to read in human terms they can understand. It's easier to digest and more productive for your company to communicate with your audience this way.

I can't tell you how many websites I've come across and still have no earthly idea what they do after reading their summary page. I've come across companies that sell VoIP telephones but have such overly complicated copy that it'd be easy to think they make some kind of NASA communications device that has absolutely nothing to do with the general public. Give that impression and the general public will think they have no business being on your site. All these companies needed to say was, "We sell telephones that operate using the Internet to make installation, use, and your bill simple."

In this day and age, simple is beautiful. There's plenty of confusion out there, so you don't need to contribute to it by crafting complex messaging that loses your prospects. Write copy that is simple and sounds human. Focus on communicating with your audience in a way that makes sense. Don't use jargon—ever. Make your prospects' lives easier by communicating in simple terms they can understand. Do this with any video, e-mail, or promotional piece you create, and you'll see the effectiveness and the results, as they relate to sales, skyrocket.

Communicate to Impinge

When writing any copy for your company, communicate to impinge. In other words, make an impact to get through to the prospect. Don't write generic copy. Take the time to think about your prospects. What problems are they dealing with? Why did they reach out to you, or why are you having a discussion? What do they need? Think about what will communicate to them specifically.

A lot of marketing tactics these days revolve around tricking the prospects to "click here" or trying to pull them in with sneaky ads that play into curiosity but aren't genuinely interesting to the prospect—and aren't going to result in a sale. The prospect was simply curious and they clicked on the ad, so it wastes everyone's time when marketers do this. This explains why a lot of websites have such high bounce rates or why pay-per-click ads have such low conversion rates. So many companies and marketers are driven by traffic these days that it's bred an entire industry of marketers writing copy that essentially tricks the audience. Although traffic is good, it means absolutely nothing if sales are not being made. You make sales by communicating in a genuine fashion that hits on the specific needs or wants of the prospect. When done correctly, it impinges and sparks interest that can genuinely be converted into sales. So it pays off to spend some time to get to know your audience. Understand what their needs are and then communicate with that in mind. Prospects will feel like you're speaking directly to them. This should be applied to every e-mail campaign, individual e-mail, advertisement, and marketing of any kind. You can get to know your prospect a lot better from either surveying your current clients or surveying prospective clients who fit your correct audience to understand these things. You can also tally all the feedback you get from current clients or prospects, look for common denominators, and then incorporate those common themes into the communications to your prospects.

The point is, communicate on a personal level that digs into the needs or wants of the audience in order for it to impinge. This will improve the likelihood of receiving an authentic response from the prospect that you can then convert to a sale.

Focus on Help

As it relates to all of your marketing and sales efforts, focus on help. That's your number one job. Not to pitch prospects and sell them something they don't need but to help them with whatever product or service you sell. When you keep this closely in mind, marketing and sales efforts become much easier. How are you helping prospects and why? What do they need help with? Help is the first thing to address and needs to be at the core of your marketing efforts. If you're just pitching a product to sell, the message comes across as empty. No one likes to just be sold something. Every prospect you ever come across has a problem he or she is trying to solve and needs help—so help. Communicate that help in your message and through all your marketing materials. You'll find your prospects are a lot more receptive and will better communicate with you.

Why Illusions Help Solidify Sales

Everything about your company communicates in one form or another—your website, your office, the way the phone is answered, the pictures on your wall, your social media sites, your blog, and so on. These items make up the illusion you create and put out as a company. In other words, they determine what people see and what they think. Illusions become the new reality. Take the time to spend a portion of your marketing efforts strictly on the illusion you create and put out there. You want your prospects to come across information about your company and think what you want them to think. If stability in your industry is a big plus point, then you should have press releases about your stability with statistics, the name of your blog should be related to stability and filled with posts that align with that topic, your Twitter page should be designed with stability built into the branding and tweets that reflect that message, the look and feel of your office should communicate that it's a stable environment, and so forth. I've always said that illusions make up 50 percent of the sale. With that said, if you don't take the time to paint your illusions, you may be losing up to 50 percent of your opportunities, meaning lost revenue. Like it or not, people buy into illusions and adopt them as reality. A lot of companies can be cheap in this department, but it's not actually being cheap; it's being wasteful, and it's costing the company a fortune. Any way you look at it, you will spend money in that area—either losing it or making they. Take good care of the illusions you put out, and they will make the money back many times over.

On Management

Increasing Production by Defining What to Do

It's of course important to be productive day to day, but I have found that the step before production or execution is the real secret—the actual planning of what needs to be done prior to doing it. If you can create a clear list of target goals that are doable or executable, you can then simply execute them. It wastes so much production time to attempt to hustle and "be productive" without fully visualizing what needs to be done and why, and then defining in writing the doable steps to be completed. When I say doable steps, I mean it's written in an actionable format. Here is an example:

1. Pick up the phone and call Mr. Peterson to discuss proposal.
2. Create the proposal as discussed for ABC Corp. and e-mail it to John.

The preceding two steps are both actions that can be done easily. If you break down your daily and weekly goals and targets and think them through, defining exactly what individual actions need to be taken, from there all you need to do is execute. That's when genuine speed, efficiency, and productivity start to happen. This simple action will make your life easier and will speed up production, allowing you to get more done.

Knowledge and Management

As the saying goes, "Knowledge is power." By *knowledge* I mean knowing your business with measurements and numbers. Many businesses or businesspeople simply go to work each day and apply effort and "work hard," making some gains some days and losing ground others. But in the end, no real progress is made. Goal attainment and progressive forward motion are not about working hard, buckling down, and trying to do better than yesterday. It comes down to knowing your business—knowing the actual numbers—so that you can correctly estimate and direct actions that will factually improve those numbers. For example, if you own a retail business, you would need to figure out the hard numbers that relate to the following:

1. How many promotional e-mails, letters, or postcards do you need to send to make one person walk through your door?
2. How many people need to walk through the door to make one sale?
3. What is the average price of one sale?
4. What is the average cost of one sale?

You get the idea. The point is, there are numbers in any business that you as a manager, executive, or owner must know. Once you know them, you can start making real progress. With the previous example, if the retail owner knew the answers to the preceding questions, she could accurately estimate her promotions, sales, and costs, and predict outcomes. Take the movie *Moneyball* as an example. Billy Beane used statistics and numbers to predict how players would score and how the outcome of games based on statistics related to each player and to all of the players combined. So with the right numbers and the right stats, you can predict next moves, what targets to set, and what the outcomes will be based on executing her strategy using the numbers that she knew.

It can be difficult to discover the fundamental numbers of a business, but it's a crucial element to making forward progress and confidently growing the company. Without these numbers, your company will flounder, with good days and bad days, ups and downs, no real accurate insight into what actually makes the company tick.

Every business has fundamental numbers that can be discovered and measured to create facts that can be managed to control outcomes and future growth. You have to "know" your company through numbers to gain traction. If you know that you have to have 10 sales discovery phone calls to make one sale, one sale is worth $10,000, and your first quarter goal is $200,000, then you know that you will need to have your sales team set up 200 sales discovery appointments in the first quarter. If you knew that it took 100 e-mails to set up one discovery sales call, you would know that you will need to send 20,000 e-mails to make that happen. It starts to give you an idea of the actual effort needed to move the company forward and grow.

Not knowing this stuff means having no control over the future of the company, and it results in missed targets or goals. Why bother having any planning meetings for the new year or the quarter if you don't have these numbers pegged? I read a great quote one time: "The best way to predict the future is to create it." You can create your future for your company by knowing the vital numbers cold. From there you can accurately predict, manage, and control your outcome.

Contraction and Expansion

When you expand at a large level in a short amount of time after a lot of hard work, push through, and eventual attainment of your expansion goals, it's natural for some level of contraction to follow immediately. It doesn't have to, of course. There are ways to quickly stabilize and increase the expansion even further, but don't get beat up by the contraction should it occur. Rather, use the time to evaluate what flaws or weaknesses the expansion helped reveal, define what the new expansion goals are, reorganize and reenergize the team, and implement systems and operations that help bolster the current level as well as allow for the new level you plan to expand to.

This constant ebb and flow of expansion and contraction continues while you grow. It's natural. There's no need to freak out about it. Just ensure that you organize behind all expansion to stabilize the growth and help contribute to new levels of expansion. Otherwise, the contraction will stick, and the entire activity becomes a little shaky, which hurts your momentum.

Use the contraction to quickly identify what needs to be addressed, address it, plan for new expansion, and hit the ground hard to push the next major targets through to completion. You will find that even your contractions leave you better off than your previous highest ever expansion levels. As long as the overall stats in the area are trending up, just keep doing this over and over to handle both expansion and contraction accordingly.

Order and Expansion

Over the past few weeks I've been on a mission to put order into every single area of our company, meaning I am making it orderly, implementing systems, and so on. The magic of "order" is limitless. Each area that we've put order into results in improvement in the company overall. In other words, we made our company more orderly in one area and found that it impacted our growth just that much for the week.

Look around your company and make a list. Find every single area that you can put order in. Then, simply address them one by one.

Here are a few examples:

- Make all work spaces neat and tidy to improve production.
- Make a revision to a contract to ensure it reads correctly.
- Address some old "need to get done" tasks and do them.
- Implement a new checklist to help make a process more efficient and swift.
- Get rid of a redundant task or function that causes needless work.

These are just a few areas. Start by listing all the areas that you want to make orderly and then do so. You will be completely blown away at how this will impact your sales, growth, expansion, morale—the list goes on.

Shed Duties

As an executive or owner—or really anyone in the company—if you are taking on more than one role with multiple duties, you need to focus on shedding them. When I say "shed," I mean you need to clearly define exactly what it is you are doing outside of your own basic role. Write down every aspect of what those other roles are and list every element of what you are doing as you cover those roles. Think about what's involved with those other duties and their corresponding role.

As an example, if you are the chief executive officer (CEO) and you are also handling sales and marketing, break those duties up and write down exactly what you are doing for the marketing role versus the sales role. What is the goal? What is the purpose? What are the daily duties? What are the daily actions or weekly tasks? Write it all down. Give examples or take screen shots if they'll help clarify. You need to take on the viewpoint of the reader, who has no idea what you're doing. You need to think like a teacher. Write a full description and then create a checklist for someone to study from start to finish. Title it something like Marketing Director Pack. You can then take this to Kinko's or a similar printing shop and have a bound training pack created.

A lot of business books and material talk about delegation, but it's pointless unless you do this. You can make your life easier by creating a training pack and hiring someone to fill that role, handing that person the pack, and telling him or her to study it, start to finish. Then you can truly delegate because each employee will now know what needs to be done and how to do it, and they will all have the written pack to refer back to instead of asking you to explain the same thing several times or risk making a critical mistake because they're not sure of what to do. Successful delegation by following these steps is truly the only way to grow your company.

As the saying goes, "If you want something done, do it yourself." This became true only because no one ever took the time to put everything down on paper so no one could hand it over and officially train other people what to do. We have done this in our agency with every position in the company to date, and it's a true game changer. Since we started doing this, our agency has quadrupled in size and revenue.

People

The essence and core of your business is people. People are the very core of everything you do as a company. They are what makes it all work, what makes it go. Therefore, much of your resources should be devoted to supporting your people.

This may mean providing training, ensuring help is available, paying bonuses, and creating a nice work environment. In other words, treat your people well. Take care of them. Help them grow. People are amazing. They are talented, smart, and innovative. People are willing and ready to play the game of winning. Acknowledge them. Support them, and most important, put them in the right place, challenge them, and allow them to grow and flourish in your company. If you put them in an area, trust them to do the job. Don't do them the disservice of handling their problems for them. Let them solve them; they're smarter than you think. I encourage you to look at doing whatever is needed this week and, from here on out, figure out how to help and service your people so that they can flourish. Provide training, challenge, and rewards.

Figure out what they need and what you can do to help them perform better. People, if you let them, can do incredible things for you and your company. Trust them and push them to blossom to their full potential and you will see the amazing effects this will have on your company.

What Makes a Group

The ultimate pursuit in business is to attain a group, a true team, loyal, focused, and driven to attain the goals of the group. It's fantastically difficult to attain but virtually indestructible once it's created.

Here are the makings of a group as I see it:

1. Everyone is focused on an agreed-upon goal. In other words, there's a mountain, and everyone sees it and is

focused on climbing it without any deviations or distractions. The goal needs to be completely known by everyone in the group and intertwined into everyday actions, targets, and programs. "What will we do today to take the mountain?" Set a goal, make it known, and pursue it.

2. The group thinks in the future, meaning that everyone in the group is focused on their future within the group. Where will we be in 2 years, 5 years, 20 years, . . . ? This then breeds loyalty to the group and therefore strengthens the group as a whole. A great group is one that no one would ever want to leave.

3. The group works as a unit, synchronizing every action and coordinating efforts. No individuals are in the group operating on a separate agenda. There is only one unit and it operates as a unit, knowing and acting in unison with every area, division, and department fully reliant on and responsible for each other.

4. There is no internal chatter about another group member in a derogatory way. Any person who seeks to bring down another within the group is immediately ousted.

5. Everyone in the group plays to his or her strengths and covers others' weaknesses to push the group forward and be strong as a group.

6. The group encourages, acknowledges, and pushes one another forward to move toward the goal.

7. The group has a set of rewards and penalties for hitting targets and missing targets that is agreed upon and known.

8. The group treats the goal as a game and plays the game to win. Let's not be bashful here; the goal is to win. Second place is as good as last place.

9. The group thinks big and sets large targets to become the elite in their field. The group also doesn't allow anyone to think small and set tiny targets that are undesirable. If we're going to go after it, let's go after the entire cake. Let somebody else set targets for slices that they don't even eat.

10. Everyone in the group acts and operates as complete professionals. There is no tolerance for amateurs who cause problems and cause the group to have setbacks. Only professionals make it in a real group, and the group members expect the very best performance out of each group member.

That to me is 10 criteria of a powerful group that would overcome any obstacle or barrier. Our agency seeks to attain these 10 points daily in order to become a fierce competitor in the global business playing field. To me, people are the essence of business and the very fiber of a group as listed previously. If you can attain a real group that operates this way and works together, then anything is achievable. One of the senior goals of your company should be to create a real group. Figure that out, and you have the keys to prosperity.

Get Rid of Bad Apples

It goes without saying that you need to remove bad apples from the company, but many organizations leave them in the ranks far too long and don't have a real method of spotting and removing them. Pay close attention to anyone who is making a lot of noise in the group or consuming a lot of management's attention. Also make note of anyone who talks a good game but doesn't seem to get any measurable results that are in a viable range. Look for complainers or people who disrupt or distract others a lot. Once you pay close attention and start to actually look for bad apples, it gets easy to spot them. Take notes of any observations related to a person you have a suspicion about. If you find that the person has very little or no personal production, makes a lot of noise, complains and distracts others or consumes management's time, get rid of him or her—and fast. You don't want to waste any time with these people. They are sapping your production and hurting morale. Your first responsibility is to the overall health and well-being of the group, not any single individual. Get the bad apples out as fast and as efficiently as possible, and you will see the group return to a pleasant and, most important, productive state.

Remove Nonproducers off the Line

Not everyone is going to be a great producer all the time. Life has a way of getting in the way sometimes, even with your most capable people. So you need to adopt a system to handle anyone who gets stuck in terms of personal production. We have a system in our agency to remove nonproducers from their daily position temporarily and send them to our training department to address any issues they're having. From there, we can have our quality control director and training director meet with them to find out what the problem is and handle it accordingly. This usually results in a write-up for that person for specific actions he or she will need to take. The person is then assigned training instructed to restudy the training pack for his or her position or the specific material related to that person's position. This is done until the issue seems to be handled and the person is confident and ready to get back to work.

There's no point in leaving nonproducers in their positions. They're jammed and need help. No level of motivation or management demand is going to change that, and if not addressed, it will ultimately lead to that person being let go, which isn't an ideal situation for anyone involved. Since we have spent huge sums of time creating training packs with material related to each position in the company, we can easily take nonproducers off their positions for the day (or for as long as it takes), have them undergo training until the issues are handled, and then get them back on their positions so that they can start being productive again. There's no need for management to get a headache over these situations. Just develop a training center and program, and assign any staff member who is hopelessly stuck or unproductive to training. This will save many good people and save the company a lot of money in the process.

True and Accurate Management

If I was forced to guess what one of the biggest downfalls of any management team or executive is, I would say it relates to misestimating numbers or actually making decisions and executing actions based on inaccurate information.

Entrepreneurs, owners, and most executives tend to be optimistic, as they should be, about future growth and goals. In many ways, you have to be optimistic to be in management. There's nothing wrong with shooting for the moon, but when it comes to information related to management decisions and actions, your data or information needs to be as accurate, precise, and real as possible.

It's vital to ensure that your team is getting you the most relevant and accurate information available. Why? Because you need to know exactly where you stand in order to make good judgment calls and set targets that will forward your goals. I've seen this become a problem in companies where executives are presented with slightly skewed numbers that are a little optimistic. People want the numbers in the company to be good, and they personally want to look good, which causes people to sometimes fluff the numbers and make them look a little better than they actually are. People don't like to confront bad news or down-trending numbers, so they present numbers or information that is slightly off (usually on the high side). This then deceives management and causes inaccurate orders and estimations.

Then, of course, management sets targets and goals as well as orders based on the slightly padded numbers, thinking they are accurate, and the company somehow "misses" the numbers. Now, this isn't always due to bad information; it can also be lack of push through or execution, but I would be willing to bet that a huge percentage of it has to do with the management team working with misinformation.

To succeed as an executive or management team, you have to be honest with yourself and ask that your team and your juniors be honest with you as well. Make sure that "feel good" numbers are never used as vital information to manage, set goals and targets, or execute. Save the overly positive numbers and information for the public relations division. You must insist that the numbers you are fed are as real and accurate as possible so that you have the exact data you need to make intelligent decisions and grow the company based on your goals, targets, and orders being set accurately.

It doesn't help anyone by having fluffed numbers or misinformation, and the "feel good" aspect of it is short-lived compared with the aftereffect of being disappointed by being off target. So be ruthless about accurate data and information, be honest with yourself, and have your team be honest with you when it comes to data or information that will be used to set targets, goals, and orders so that you can accurately attain your goals and everyone can take a win when you do.

On People

Client Needs, Not Wants

Recently we had a situation at our agency that reminded me of the importance of delivering what clients need rather than what they may think they want. Although clients play a major role in decisions and influence your company's actions—mostly because every company is trying to please their clients and keep them happy to create long-term relationships—the truth is that many times, to actually please clients and deliver the results, you must focus on what the clients need rather than what they are saying they want.

Let me clarify. A client requests you change your strategy because he or she has a few ideas that they want to include and really focus on. You then deviate off of the path that you absolutely know works and know gets results in an effort to serve the client and address his or her wants. The results then reflect the deviation off course from what you know you should have done. And not surprisingly, because you've deviated from what actually does work, the client is not happy, which is bad for business.

Had you held your position and sold and delivered the client on what you knew was successful, what gets results, and what was really what the client needed, you would ultimately end up with a happy client and a great long-term relationship.

Focus on what you do as a company that you know works and gets results, identify what the client really needs to address a problem, and then aggressively sell and deliver only that. Sticking to your guns and delivering a product or service that handles your client's actual needs (assuming you have correctly identified them) will guarantee you positive results and happy clients. Handle your clients' needs only and don't be persuaded to deviate to focus on wants that you know will take the strategy off course, with results that will not be the desired outcome.

As the saying goes, "Find a need; fill a need."

How to Handle Critical Clients

In business, it's truly inevitable that you will run into problems that result in critical clients. We've found there are two ways to handle a complaint or critical client as it relates to our agency:

1. Take the complaint or critical remark at face value and honestly inspect what is being complained about. Do not immediately push back on the client in an attempt to make yourself "right." Investigate to see if you made an error or one of your people made a mistake. If you discover that you have, fix it immediately and turn the complaint into an opportunity to expand and get better at what you do. Every critical

statement or complaint has an opportunity attached to it. If you can use the critical remarks to strengthen your company, then take advantage of it.

2. If the client seems to be the type that complains about everything or is just critical in general, burn that relationship. In other words, resign the client—and fast. Don't keep critical clients around; they lower company morale, which lowers production and therefore creates more problems for the company as a whole. We never keep clients that are critical and hurt the company morale. Keep only clients that are essentially working as a team with your company to solve problems and that are pleasant to deal with. I promise, this one rule will help expand your company tenfold.

No one likes getting complaints or dealing with a critic, but if you apply the preceding two rules, you can turn both situations into an opportunity to expand your company. Give it a go.

Customers Aren't Always Right

I realize that most people in business have heard or have been trained on the concept that "the customer is always right," but it's a trap for your business and not a long-range strategy or operating basis that you should subscribe to.

The truth is, it was you that came up with your business idea. You have created it every day and worked out the kinks—not your customer. Customers don't always know what they need or want until you actually present it to them. Although it is very important to listen to customers to understand their needs or problems, it doesn't mean it's a good idea to take every suggestion or to listen to their ideas on how to operate your company.

Your job is to solve their problem. Stick to what you do and to your ideas for how to accomplish that. Become intimately familiar with customers' problems and then work out the solutions based on your own insights, knowledge, and experience to attain what's needed. After all, if the customer knew everything about how to solve their own problems, they wouldn't be coming to you! If you operate on the premise that the customer is always right, I can almost guarantee that this will lead you off your course and down a dark path that you shouldn't be traveling. You've built an entire company based on what you have come up with—your ideas, your methods—and the customer signed up because of it. Deal with any suggestions or complaints as they come up, sure. But don't deviate off course based on listening to everything the customer says, or you'll find that one day your progress slows or declines because you've been changing your company based on the false idea that the customer is always right.

Know your company. Know your clients' problems and have total faith in the methods you use to solve them—and stick to what you know is workable. Continue to improve your company to solve the problem better but don't get distracted by customer input, ideas, or complaints. If you solve the problem, get good at doing what you do, and consistently improve based on what you know, you won't need to worry about customers' input because they will be extremely pleased with what you have done.

Here's a great quote from Steve Jobs, former chief executive officer (CEO) of Apple, that relates to this:

> You can't just ask customers what they want and then try to give that to them. By the time you get it built, they'll want something new.

So focus your efforts. Improve your systems and delivery for what you do, but ultimately you have to know your company's goals and purpose, who you are, and what you are trying to be. That will carve your company into the ideal vision you are trying to attain. Customers don't know what the vision is or how to get there. And they never will, so focus on doing what you do and servicing them better to handle their problems, needs, or wants. This will ensure that everyone will be happy.

The Best Time to Fire Them Is Before You Hire Them

While people are your greatest asset, they can also be your greatest headache.

The truth is, good people are your greatest asset, but bad people within your group can be very destructive and can dramatically slow your growth. I've always said that the best time to fire is before you hire. This isn't to say that you need to be so strict that you don't let anyone in, because that will hurt your growth. You must hire to grow, but you need to be smart. You need to write down key criteria of what an ideal candidate should be for your company.

Over the years, we've defined a Richter-type employee. We know what we're looking for, which makes interviews easy. We assess possible new hires based on their attitude, willingness, communication level, interest in what we do, relative aptitude for what we do, and eagerness to get started. We focus on qualities that will allow people to easily mesh with our company and candidates who we can easily train for the specific skill of the job. We then assess, based on their personality and characteristics, where we need to put them within our company based on where we believe they will excel.

In my opinion, résumés are worthless. Candidates can say anything, and the résumés are generally fluffed. If you rely on a résumé, you're shooting yourself in the foot. It's not a smart play. You need to hone your skills at spotting candidates who will work well on your team. I throw résumés in the garbage—never read them and never will.

Instead, make an outline of what you're looking for in a candidate and define all of the criteria. Then stick to it. Have interviews and ask questions about what they like to do businesswise, what they know about your company, why they are interested, where they believe they would fit best, and so on. Don't stick to the generic interview questions because (1) they don't work, and (2) the candidate most likely studied the answers and is ready with fluff.

You want genuine answers so you can gauge their communication level. How fast do they reply? Is it authentic? Do they know anything about your company?

Are they interested in the company, or are they just looking for a job? We don't hire people just looking for a "job." We hire people who like what we do, are genuinely interested, and want to be a part of our group.

By being smart about the way you hire, you can filter out the people who won't fit upfront and then bring in only the people who have a good shot at making it within your company. The traditional interviewing methods aren't working, as evidenced by the large number of personnel problems in most workplaces. So we need to stop doing silly things like reading résumés and asking canned interview questions. We need to look for authentic criteria that lead to hiring the very best people for a company. I suppose over the years we've gotten lazy and lost the ability to clearly assess people, which is why we now rely on things like résumés, but we need to get back to basics to reestablish our ability to simply assess character and common elements that will suit the company's needs.

Criticism and Considerations

With regard to your people, you need to let them know that they should write down anything they don't like, feel critical about, or have a negative or positive consideration (thought) about. They should then send that written comment to the appropriate senior person relevant to their area. *Do not* allow people to communicate it out loud and begin discussions with their colleagues about the topic. Communicating critical remarks or considerations to colleagues works as a counterintention to the group. This hurts stats overall, both for the person making the remarks and for the group. It's fantastically unproductive and destructive to the company.

Instead, if an employee is unhappy about anything at all, the correct action is to have that person write it down, via e-mail or on paper, and send it to the correct person to address it immediately.

It is crucial to give people an avenue to clear the air and handle any situations in the company, but don't allow for people to vent in the open. The matter can become explosive. Create a simple procedure for how to handle this sort of situation and let everyone on the team know what it is. In some companies, employees place their handwritten notes into small boxes and management then reads those weekly and handles issues as needed. Do whatever works for you. Just don't let things fester and don't let people vent in the open.

On Being Promoted

You have to set your terms when it comes to promotion within the company for two reasons:

1. It gives people a goal to work toward.
2. It sets the rules for how promotions are handled so that there's no chance for politics or cliques.

At Richter we have a specific outline that sets the terms for our people. We let our people know that all promotions will be treated as new interviews for the positions and the best candidates will be chosen.

Here's an outline of our terms:

- *Performance:* We measure performance of all of our people with statistics, and this plays a central role in our decision to give a promotion. We look for people who consistently perform for their areas, which can be visually seen per their statistic graphs.
- *Attitude:* The person wanting to be promoted must exhibit a good attitude in his or her current role and at the company in general. This attitude must be clearly seen and acknowledged. This includes being interested in the work, our company, and the people with whom we work.
- *Consistency:* The person must show a consistent work schedule and have statistics that show consistent production with little correcting or debugging needed.
- *Problem Solving:* The person must show an ability to identify and intelligently solve problems within his or her current role. He or she must also get the results for his or her post with very little guidance from direct seniors.
- *Work Ethic:* The person must exhibit a strong work ethic that shows on his or her post. This includes being professional and working hard to execute all actions related to the person's post, such as driving his or her statistics, hitting assigned targets, achieving quotas and goals, having a high responsibility for the position and taking it seriously, and working hard to ensure that it is running smoothly.

These are a few points that we weigh and balance to gauge how we promote someone. You may have different internal criteria, but the point is to define what that criteria are and make them known to your people. Knowing what you're looking for, they can then effectively work toward a promotion as a goal.

On Viewpoint

Aim Small, Miss Small

There was a line in the movie *The Patriot* where the character Mel Gibson plays is about to ambush a group of British soldiers to save his son. He tells his other two sons to remember what he has taught them: "Aim small, miss small."

The other day I was in a meeting with our production team, and while we were discussing strategies to attain "client reaches" (this is our coined term for relationships that we have developed for our clients which are reaching toward an ideal sales opportunity for our client), that exact phrase came out of my mouth: "Aim small, miss small."

It's a great concept and relates directly to business and client growth. Focus your efforts. In other words, identify a segment you want to go after by profiling whom you sell to now. Who actually buys from you, as opposed to an idealized client to whom you have yet to sell anything? Then take aim at that small segment and go after them heavily. We are not aiming at the whole audience here; we are aiming at your audience—the people most likely to need, want, and buy your products or services.

Why waste your time, effort, money, and energy chasing the entire audience, many of whom will most likely never buy from you anyway. Focus. Aim small, miss small. Define the audience and go after them. You will "miss" a few within that audience, meaning you won't sell or close them, but you will "hit" a lot of them. I can guarantee you that the small audience you aim for actually makes up a huge number, which is most likely more than your company could ever take on as clients.

Busy or Disorganized

Okay, this one may push a few people's buttons, but I thought I should write it anyway. I frequently hear the word "busy" in business and felt the need to address this and challenge others to be honest with themselves.

I personally happen to be a very organized person, but even I fall behind from time to time and need to pick up the slack to catch up and stay on track. I don't blame it on "busy" though; I blame it on me being disorganized and not staying focused and handling my cycles one at a time until they are done, done, done.

We all have the same amount of time in the day and we are all "busy," but that's not an excuse to let anything slide. Besides, the people you are telling that you are "busy" don't buy it anyway.

So call it what it is—lack of organization—and get organized. Without organization, you're simply not getting your tasks done on time, wasting time during the day, or being inefficient. Organized and productive business-people can get a spectacular amount of work done in a day. While you're blaming your disorganization on being busy, your competition and prospective clients, whom you can't seem to get around to, are out-tasking you or bypassing you altogether, with the only possible long-term outcome being decline for your organization and for you as an individual.

My challenge to you is to stop using the excuse of being too busy and simply call it what it is: disorganization. Then address it for what it is and work toward a genuine solution. How can you get more organized? How can you be more efficient during the day? How can you get more done? Focus on ways to handle your organizational problems, such as using a daily targets plan and checking off each task as you get it done, or not multitasking but rather simply focusing on completing the task at hand before going to the next and the next and the next—a sort of "Get it done, handle it now, what's next?" type of system.

If you are honest with yourself on this, you will agree that you are not nearly as busy as you're claiming; you're simply disorganized. The great news is that once you confront this and take some simple steps to improve your personal level of organization, you'll find you can get way more done than you might have thought possible. In addition, your personal stress level will decrease in direct proportion to your increased productivity and organization.

Here are a few ways you could be more organized:

1. Make a daily agenda with targets for the day that must be hit.
2. Handle each target daily one by one, completing each one fully before putting any attention on the next.

This can take some getting used to, as we're all accustomed to having our attention pulled in a dozen different directions at once and thinking of that as productivity. In reality, being able to finish a particular task completely then frees up your attention to focus on the next task, making you much more productive and probably saving your sanity in the process.

3. Schedule and/or budget your time on your calendar to make sure you are being fully productive with your day.

4. Stop engaging in activities that waste time during the day, such as chitchatting with others in the office, browsing the Web aimlessly, and jumping from task to task and not fully completing any of them.

5. Check your e-mail only after a task is done. That is, fully complete a target and only then check e-mail. Address any messages and then go back and work on the next target until it is fully done.

6. Don't accept interruptions. Tell people you are in the middle of a task and will come see them as soon as it is completed. Then do so and go back to the next target right after.

These simple steps will help immensely. I also recommend that you make a list of all of the ways you are being disorganized or inefficient during the day, then fully confront each one and handle all of them appropriately.

Time is precious. Why waste it and get stuck into indefinite busy mode? Your personal livelihood and that of your organization depend on you being as productive as possible. And nothing is more satisfying in business than accomplishing a task successfully all the way through to the end. Organization = sanity. The more organized you are, the more you can get done, the more you can take on, and the more you effectively control your environment.

Dreams and Goals

Each year on my birthday, I think about dreams and goals. To me, when I view life as if through a telescope, the purpose, reason, and so on, all boil down to dreams and goals. Think about it for a second. What are we doing here on Earth? What's the purpose? I don't mean to get mystical here, but it's interesting to put it all in perspective once in a while.

Life is simple. You make dreams, set goals to attain those dreams, and then execute to make it all happen. When you attain goals, and therefore dreams, you make new dreams and set new goals. Maybe you dream of having a family that you take care of and grow with, or maybe your dream is to learn to scuba dive and then go to the Cayman Islands to do so. It doesn't matter what your dreams are; it only matters that you have them. People get lost from time to time or seem directionless and make life too complex in the process.

Life is about your dreams and goals and the pursuit of making them realities. Make it a point to dream dreams, set goals, and go after them daily, weekly, monthly, and yearly. And then follow up on your dreams and goals to check your progress. Never stop creating dreams and goals to attain; it's the very essence of life itself.

I heard a saying once that went like this, "There are only two tragic situations in life—someone who has nothing and someone who has everything." This, to me, relates to someone who has no dreams or goals and someone who has attained his or her dreams and goals and neglected to make new ones. Life is about living, and you do that through dreaming dreams, making goals, and going after them.

Focus

The other day I was going through my Twitter feed and saw a tweet asking a question to Gurbaksh Chahal (a very successful entrepreneur who sold his last company for $300 million and the one before it for $40 million) about whether he gets tempted to work on other ideas while he is working on a company. His response? "Never. Focus is everything."

To me one of the biggest elements of failure—or simply lack of success—lies in most people's lack of ability to stay focused. I'll admit, I love millions of ideas as well and have a tendency to daydream from time to time. But since I have owned four companies, I know the power of focused attention and the deadliness of distractions or dispersals. Focus is everything.

If you know what your company stands for, sells, and delivers; have clearly named or defined your product or service; and then defined your goal or vision, the only next step for you to take is to do only those things that are focused toward executing the goals to attain the vision.

Do not get distracted and do not let any other "bright ideas" enter the equation. Focus your time, energy, and effort on your goal.

The analogy I would use is the one about chasing rabbits: if you are trying to chase two rabbits at the same time, you'll end up with none. On the other hand, if you select one to focus on and go after it, there's a good chance you will catch it.

Don't try to be everything to everyone. Know who you are and what you do and do it well. Get focused and develop tunnel vision to work toward attaining your goals. Stomp out distractions the second they come up, including any new bright ideas that "potentially could make a whole lot of money." Just focus and perfect what you are doing and do it well. That is the road to long-term, stable success and prosperity.

What You Did Yesterday Doesn't Matter

It's a tough fact to swallow for most, but the truth is, what you did yesterday really doesn't matter in business. People sometimes have the tendency to try to justify today's lack of performance by using yesterday's actions or results. The reality is that businesses operate by the minute—right now and in the future. What did you do today? What do you have lined up or planned for tomorrow?

My dad's business partner used to always say, "Make a good deal today or execute a good idea today. Don't wait for the perfect deal tomorrow because tomorrow never comes." So the focus is on today. Don't use yesterday's success or results to get complacent today. Yesterday doesn't justify today's lack of performance. Judge yourself every day. Push yourself to perform every day. It's a daily discipline that will pay off big over time.

Second Wind

Everybody swings up and down in life. Some days you're on top of your game and others . . . not so much. In business, as in any sport or activity, you need to really zero in on what gives you your second wind—in other words, whatever takes the time out of the equation for you to bounce back, allowing you to get your game face on and continue your forward momentum.

For me, it's reading and running. When my thoughts seem a little unclear and I'm a little beat up by the week or need to address the various "urgent" problems that arose in the business, I go for a run or I read. Reading gives me clarity. I read mostly business books because they help exercise my thoughts and allow clear ideas to circulate in my mind, ideas that almost always help me handle the exact issues I'm faced with in my company. Running allows me to completely focus my attention outward rather than inward. Bodies need exercise, and pushing yourself to the limit physically will give you a feeling of calm and clarity. While running, I am able to clear my mind and think of new ideas to address various problems as well.

You have to find what works for you. How can you get your second wind? For you, it might be shopping or taking a short trip out of town. Whatever it may be, figure it out and do it every time you get the wind knocked out of you a little so you can get back on your game and on your mission to attain your goals.

Isn't It a Sport?

We all agree that practice makes perfect. Training is directly related to winning, and in sports, competence from training and practice makes all the difference in the world. So it would make sense to apply the same principles to business, wouldn't it? Business runs on the same principles as any sport or game: rules, strategies, opponents, goals, scores, and so on. But how many people take business as seriously when it comes to training and practice? What are you currently doing to get better at what you do?

I heard that prior to winning the Masters Tournament, Vijay Singh dedicated a tremendous amount of time to practicing every shot. It seems the same logic applies in business. To become the best at what you do, you need to study, train, and practice. This could mean reading, taking courses, drilling, reviewing all current stats to understand the existing scene, going to events, seeing speakers, and so on. It could be anything that you believe helps you measurably improve the way you operate. Everyone needs to spend time training, studying, and practicing to get better at what they do. Without constant learning or practice to improve yourself, you get stale and mechanical. Take your business and profession seriously. Learn to improve. Study. Train and practice what you do by whatever means necessary. You'll never excel and improve on your year-over-year results without an effective training strategy. Don't allow yourself to become complacent. Business, like any sport, requires a huge focus on training and practice to stay sharp, improve results, and ultimately win at whatever it is you're doing.

Be Honest with Yourself

The value of honesty in business is clear, but the value of being honest with yourself is critical. We've all done it. We've failed to be honest with ourselves about various situations in business that, left unaddressed, become thorns in our sides. This dishonesty with ourselves comes from our desire to believe things are better than they are or to believe that the person who we know deep down is not working out will somehow magically improve. Or it could be simply that we don't want to confront the reality of a specific situation. There are countless situations in business that come up and are ultimately awkward for you and others, but the truth is the truth and as such it's ultimately unavoidable. You know it in your gut and not doing anything about it or trying to change it . . . well . . . won't change anything. Be honest with yourself. Address things candidly and look at the actual situation; then make swift decisions based on your honest assessment. You'll find that most situations that come up in business become a lot simpler. Once you confront what's right in front of you, complex circumstances that must be handled are suddenly no longer complex.

Difficulties fester from you not confronting situations and not being honest about them as they arise. They will quickly resolve and dissipate when you are honest with yourself and promptly act on that honesty to address and remedy situations.

The Buck Stops with You

In business, as in life, the buck always stops with you. You are responsible for your outcomes. It's a hard fact for many to face. If you look at every situation in your life or business and operate on the basis that it's your responsibility and you are the master of your outcomes, it all becomes smooth sailing from there on out.

People are going to fall on their faces. How well people deal with hardship or turmoil relates to the degree that they look for external causes for their fall. Blaming some outside influence is counterproductive. It's you—always has been, always will be. Your efforts, your actions, and your decisions are the only thing you should be concerned with. Don't seek other reasons; they don't exist. You're lying to yourself and wasting your time, effort, and energy if you think otherwise.

Take full responsibility—full accountability—for the outcome of your actions and know that the buck stops with you. Once you know this and operate with it, things get better. You can control the game. You can set your strategy plan, and you can work causatively toward your goals. Knowing that it's you is empowering.

Decide to take full accountability and responsibility for all outcomes from here on out. Don't look for anything to blame for less-than-desirable outcomes, ever. With that, you can truly take charge and control the game and your goals.

Find Inspiration

Inspiration breeds action. Each day, use something that inspires you to act. Reaching goals requires taking action. If you want to get anywhere in life, you need to act. Inspiration helps action. It forces you to do, to push through barriers and execute.

What inspires you? Find things that seem to inspire you and incorporate them into your day. It could be a video, a movie, a quote, a picture, an idea, whatever. Just discover it and then use it daily to inspire action. Success and goal attainment come down to how badly you want something and then acting on your goals to execute tasks that will get you there. People have up days and down days, but if you keep yourself inspired and focused, each day can be packed with actions that move you toward your goals. Find something that inspires you and use it daily.

Staying the Course

Over the years in business, I have seen two distinct personality types as they relate to success: those who stay the course and those who jump from place to place.

Consistently I have seen the ones who stay the course in whatever path they have chosen outperform those who hop around.

Most people want success, but few have the discipline and focus to attain it. You must decide first and foremost on what you are going to commit to. Then you need to do everything to learn it, do it, hustle, get better at it, and most important, stay the course. The temptation to jump ship and do something else is a distraction. Stay the course. Focus on what you decided to do and do it well over time. This is the road to take if you want long-term success.

Let's take a few examples:

- Steve Jobs started Apple in the 1970s. He stayed focused on computers and doing what he loved doing his entire working life.
- Ralph Lauren has been interested in fashion and design since his teens; he has never deviated from this path.
- Richard Branson started the Virgin brand of companies in his early twenties. Although he owns a diverse portfolio of companies, if you ask him, he will tell you that his businesses are all composed of the same Virgin brand principles, making the overall company a "branded venture group" company.

These are just a few examples of high-profile people you may have heard of, but I know a huge number of not quite as high profile but still extremely successful people who have followed the same formula. They have focused on something they wanted to do—plastics, computers, sales, technology, hotels—and they have stayed the course their entire working lives. On the other hand, I haven't met too many people who jump around from one place to the next who are successful. In all honesty, I haven't met one.

So the takeaway here is this:

1. Find something you want to do forever and decide to do it.
2. Stay the course and persist to attain success in that field despite any barriers and obstacles that may present themselves.

Dragging Decisions Is Bad Business

Too frequently in business you hear people say, "Let me get back to you next week," "Let's discuss this at the end of the third quarter," and so on. This kind of procrastination related to making decisions is bad business. The decision or information at hand will not change in two months, next week, or next year. No decision is perfect. Keep in mind that the decisions you make are critical, and the faster you can make them and implement them, the better. Force yourself to look at the situation, evaluate the opportunities, and make a decision right now.

Every delay you make hurts your business. Your slowness or inability to make fast decisions is holding you back. Learn to discipline yourself to make fast decisions and commit to those decisions in order to speed up the flow of your company. Watch what happens when this is implemented. Swift decisions and swift actions will lead to growth and success. Let your competition mess around with delayed decision-making processes but don't allow yourself to fall into the habit of it.

Adding Time

How much time is added unnecessarily to your life? Just imagine for a second how many situations in your business time gets added into when it didn't need to be. Here are a few examples to exercise your thoughts:

- You get an e-mail and instead of handling it right then and there, you put it away for "later."
- You tell someone in business that you will review and handle this "next week" when you could handle it right now.
- You don't gather all the people who need to be associated with a decision immediately to put it to bed right now, only to procrastinate and put it off for another day.
- You defer a decision to someone else when you can actually handle it and be done with it.

These are just a few examples, but imagine if you made a list of every occasion where you added time to a situation that didn't require it and then you stopped doing it! A lot of time would be freed up for you. A ton of time actually. So it isn't really that you never have enough time, is it? No. It's that you gobble up all the available time you have with the fluff of "adding time" to various situations for no apparent reason. Stop doing it and buy yourself extra time to get more done. You will be amazed at how much you are actually capable of. Let your competition or other folks add time, but don't join them in this idiotic and expensive activity.

Decision Comes First

Decision seems to be a relatively misunderstood word. In business, people talk about decisions, the decision maker, and so forth, but they rarely truly understand the power of decisions and the priority they take in getting anything done.

Many people try to have all the facts and information lined up prior to making a decision, or more specifically in order to make a decision. It doesn't work like that.

It works like this: you have to look at what you want to do and then decide and commit to what you'll do to achieve the desired outcome. Make a decision that is unwavering. Then work toward the decision, taking actions to execute what you decided on. This will give you the cleanest and most precise result based on your decision.

Decide. Then take actions to execute that decision.

Don't waffle and come up with option after option. No maybe this, no maybe that. Look at what you want, make a decision, and take actions toward executing your decision to make it happen. It's that simple. Focus on making clear, crisp decisions and taking actions that make those decisions your new reality.

Doubt

The most insidious infection your business can face is doubt. Seek out anyone who may be infected with it and address it head-on or get that person out of your company and quarantine the area.

Yes, it's that serious. Anyone who may have any doubts about your future, the vision of the company, and his or her belief in pulling it off is a liability. People like this will drag you down. Their doubts will infect your progress and other people—count on it. Handle them or get rid of them. Your team must be composed of enthusiastic, focused, determined, and confident people who relentlessly persist toward the goal with total belief that they will attain it. That is how you win.

If you have people on board who are doubtful, shoot them from cannons. Keeping them around makes about as much sense as keeping someone in a rowboat who is paddling in the opposite direction of everyone else. You'll end up exhausted, without having gotten anywhere. If you believe in your ability to attain your vision and get everyone to move toward that vision with total conviction, you will absolutely attain it.

Spend More Time Planning

I realize that planning can seem like a waste of time or an extra headache, but it will save you a huge amount of time and wheel spinning throughout your week.

I see a lot of people go to work, get into the motion of work, handle actions as they come, and attempt to produce with very little forward motion related to their actions. What we are looking to attain here is precise, predictable forward motion that conquers goals.

Here's what I want you to do: take time to plan your week. On Sunday, write down or type out exactly what needs to be done for the week to attain your goals. Make it clear, concise, and actionable. If you're in sales, list every cycle you are working on and the actions needed to close each cycle this week. Be thoughtful about the physical steps that must be done to execute and attain each action.

Then, when Monday comes, you simply need to execute the plan. Stick to the plan. Push the plan through. Get it done. That's it. Don't try to just "be productive" with no game plan. Be thorough, make a defined plan, and then do it. Simple. Try it out.

Simple Is Smart

People have a tendency to make things entirely too complex. I'm not sure why this is. The propaganda out there is that complex subjects and solutions are smart. If you have to think and think and "figure figure" something, well, it must be highly valuable to use up all your intelligence. That's not the case. You can save time and energy by laying out the steps and sequences to take. All situations in business can be broken down into simple terms. Although things may seem complex or a solution may appear to need a complex solution, the opposite is usually true.

It's not hard to make things seem complex. It's certainly a lot easier than making things simple. Any fool can make a problem complex or introduce a complex solution, but it takes a genius to make something simple. The ability to break something down into very simple concepts or terms that can be easily digestible and assimilated by anyone is precious in business. If you can surround yourself with people who can think simply, dissect problems, and come up with simple solutions, you will have a powerful team.

Any problem you are dealing with right this minute can be solved with a simple solution. Anyone who tells you otherwise is most likely trying to justify his or her position or salary. Simple is smart. Start looking at every problem your company is facing and figure out the simplest solution. It's typically one that hasn't been discovered because the entire team is busy searching for the "complex" problem or discussing how incredibly complicated it all is.

Every solution is simple, and in order to discover that, you will need to discipline yourself to start thinking simply. Look for the simple answers, and they will start to reveal themselves. Ask simple questions that may sound overly simplistic but that will lead to the smartest solutions. Do not trust complex solutions and do not believe people who tell you that the problem or solution is complex. These people have problems with how they think. They will create havoc within your company. Get rid of them. Focus on taking the time to discover the simple answers within your business—such as sales, public relations (PR), operations, people—and this will help lead to great growth.

Write It Down

There's a secret to success. You have to visualize where you want to be and how you plan to get there. Then, you need to write it down. There is something magic about writing. I carry a nice pen and a moleskin journal with me virtually everywhere I go. You can, of course, type things on your computer, but I'm biased in favor of pen and paper. Something magic happens when you think a thought and then write it down on paper in your journal. It can be a goal, an idea, a plan; it doesn't matter, just write it down. This is a critical step toward making things happen. I have met many successful and unsuccessful people, and I'm telling you, successful people write down their thoughts, goals, and ideas consistently. Get the vision of what you want to write clear in your mind and then just start writing. It will flow. The writing will lead to more writing. Make a habit of it. Start with things like a goals list. Think it through. Visualize it and then write it down. Then, read what you wrote. I flip through my moleskin journal at least once a week to review and scan all my notes. Look for things to remind yourself what needs to be done. As you do this, you will convert your writing to memory and start working those notes, ideas, and goals into realities. I guarantee that if you do this, you will start looking at your notes and realize, "Wow, that was done." Bit by bit you'll start to accomplish the things you write.

Writing is magic. I find it therapeutic. I can be wired from a long day or a little stressed out, and when I get home,

I pull out my journal and pen and start writing what's on my mind. I dump the complete contents of my mind and put it on paper. Once I have dumped it all, I have a feeling of calm. I also feel that I have captured my thoughts and energies on paper, which allows me to forget about them immediately. From there, I can free up my attention to focus on the next thing. People who don't write things down use their mental energy to keep track of things they don't want to forget, meaning they most likely end up with their attention stuck on those things. This is unproductive and limits your potential.

If you don't do this yet, get yourself a journal of sorts and a nice pen that you like to write with. Start writing your thoughts, ideas, goals, and dreams on paper. Then read it. Study your notes and know them. You will start to work toward making your goals realities. It's truly magic. Simple, but magic nonetheless.

You Have to Love Feeling Causative

To really win, you have to love feeling causative and, conversely, detest feeling that situations out of your command have control of you. Everything you do must lean toward being causative. In other words, you need to figure out how to control the game, how to tilt things in your favor. This isn't to say that you need to be a control freak, but you do need to know that you are the cause of everything and you must deeply desire to keep it that way. Anything that puts you at effect and takes you out of control of the situation is a nonoptimal condition that you need to handle and remove. You and your entire time have to love being causative and work toward it daily.

For example, let's say you measured everything in your company and discovered that when you send out 400 promotional e-mails, you get back 40 interested parties. Of those interested parties, you will close a deal with 25 percent. You know this because the exact sequence to handle sales of that specific product has been worked out in a flowchart that your sales manager uses to manage the sales team daily and ensure that the exact substeps needed to result in 25 percent or more sales closed are followed. You also know that each sale is worth $50,000. If you need to make $500,000 in gross sales, being causative then equates to following a very simple math equation: 400 e-mails out = 40 responses in, 10 deals closed, and $500,000 in new sales in the door.

This is just one example of one area where being completely methodical with your numbers allows you to take causative action. Many sales teams leave business on the table month in and month out or select some oddball excuse like, "Sales are down because it's August and everyone is on vacation." But the truth is that selecting some external factor as cause simply puts your company at effect, which means numbers will be missed and revenue will be lost. It's that simple. You have to love being causative and demand that the company conforms to your desire to be causative. We operate this way and recently had the highest sales in the history of our company while our competition (I use that term loosely) was complaining and making "reasonable" excuses about everyone being on vacation. We have made checklists of points where we believe we are passive and then have worked out solutions for each of those items to move us into a causative position.

Pushing Purpose

To attain anything in life or business, you must have your purpose defined. This doesn't need to be some fluffy statement that you frame for PR's sake. It needs to be real to you and your people. Figure out what it is. Why are you doing what you do? What drives you? What motivates you? Write it down as many times as it takes until you feel you have defined what the basic purpose really is. Once you have a very clear picture of this and you can read it out loud to yourself and know it to be true, then you can start working toward it as a group. So the first step is to define it. The second step is to make it known to your people and to get them to focus their actions toward attaining it. Push purpose. What I mean by that is you need to have everyone within the group know and understand the basic purpose of the company: why you do what you do or why you got into business in the first place; then you can drive all orders and actions toward it. This is a very powerful tool to achieve great things as a company. Just chasing money is an empty path. You need to push purpose in order to drive revenue and continue to push growth. Purpose will keep you going.

Take some time to figure it out and define it. Once complete, post it on your wall. Make it known in memos to your staff and assign orders that align with it. People will start to beat their drums for that purpose and at that point you will be well on your way to achieving great things.

Making Friends

It's easy in business and in sales to lose sight of what you are trying to do or the purpose behind everything, so here is a little reminder: it's about relationships. It's about people. It's about helping another person or company attain its goals, which helps you attain yours as well. It's about the *why* of what you are doing. And it's about making friends.

Business shouldn't be a grind. It's not. It's about building relationships with others that result in more business. We tend to look at sales and taking on new clients as making new friends. It may sound hokey, but the truth is I want to do business only with people whom I like and whom I'd like to deal with daily and into the future. My ideal scenario would be to have ongoing relationships with my clients so that we could develop a working friendship. Our goal is to make friends with clients. This creates the ideal setting for your business. That is how you build stability and ultimately gain the most pleasure out of what you do. Work becomes more of a game, and time with clients becomes fun.

Start looking at your client base to decide with whom you feel you can develop better relationships and how to make them more like friends. Also, consider whom you may need to get rid of as clients, perhaps because they don't align with your business. This one issue—to do business only with companies or people with whom you believe you can create long-term relationships and ultimately make your friends—can result in a huge amount of growth for your company. The foundation and strength of your company will grow from this alone. So go make some friends, not just clients.

Title versus Task

What is a title to you? Your professional title, whether it is chief executive officer (CEO), vice president (VP) of sales, creative director, or chief financial officer (CFO), what does it actually mean to you? If you're thinking it has anything to do with power or importance, then you have completely missed the mark and have lost the true purpose of your job and position within your company.

A title is not for power or importance or for making anyone feel less important or valuable than you; it's a description of where you are in your company and what your responsibilities are. It's a function. Now I realize this sounds a little self-explanatory, but many people seem to misuse and misapply their titles, which is a shame and a detriment to the organization in general.

When you are a CEO, or hold any position for that matter, that title simply is a label for your function. It means that the day-to-day tasks related to that title are your responsibility and that your team relies on you to get them done. That's it. If you thought it was anything more than that, you've lost the focus and true spirit of business.

Think about the tasks and functions that go along with your position or title. This is the only importance associated with your title. It dictates your job and reveals your tasks so that everyone knows who is who in the company and who will handle what functions. Think of your company and position like a sport: the goalie is supposed to stop attempts at scoring a goal, period. The goalie is not there so he can be respected or act important (even though he is); it's simply a duty.

Take a look at your post, position, or title and ask yourself whether you are exclusively handling your functions to support your team to help get the job done and whether you are making a valuable contribution to your team based on the responsibilities that fall under your position. If you do this, your company will perform better. And if you can get others to do the same, the company will boom.

Focus on the task at hand, the functions that need to be done per your job title and execute, execute, execute. Forget the importance of it all. The irony, of course, is that the more you do this, the more power, influence, and respect you're likely to command.

Be a Ball Hog

Have you ever heard someone say, "The ball is in their court," when explaining where a certain situation stands?

If you're a true professional and want to bend over backward to serve your client, then you will adopt the philosophy that the ball is never in your client's court.

You need to control the ball in order to control the outcome.

Fully servicing your client requires total control of each situation and task, which allows you to get the desired results you are focused on, thereby creating happy clients.

For example, you've probably had the experience of visiting an incredible hotel that truly has their delivery, service, and overall operations completely under their control. They anticipate your needs and treat you like royalty from first moment to last. The outcome is that, as a client, you are very happy and feel well taken care of, which is ultimately what every paying customer wants.

Do your clients a favor and never leave the ball in their court; they don't want it!

Being a Martinet about Neatness

I was reading a book by David Ogilvy where he tells a story about how he used to work in a professional kitchen in France. The head chef, Mr. Pitard, was a martinet (one who enforces strict discipline) about being neat. He had the chefs clean the kitchen twice per day to ensure the quarters were spotless. David carried many of these lessons over to his agency, which grew to be one the best and biggest of his time.

David's comment for his agency was this:

Today I am a martinet in making my staff keep their offices shipshape. A messy office creates an atmosphere of sloppiness, and leads to the disappearance of secret papers.

I agree fully. I am a bit of a neat freak myself and always keep my quarters shipshape. I also tend to get a lot more done than the average person, I think partly because I operate in a neat and orderly fashion. It's worth taking a look at yourself. Do you keep your office immaculate? Is everything where it should be? If not, I'm willing to bet that you are losing valuable time and opportunities.

It takes next to nothing to learn this basic discipline of being neat, which, coincidentally is a trait of many of the very successful people I've met. Practice being neat. Start making your quarters neat and tidy this week, and you will see that your level of production rises, as well as your personal sense of morale and satisfaction.

Manage Objectives Like LEGO Instructions

If you've ever put together a LEGO toy, then you've experienced simplicity at its best. LEGO has done a fantastic job at breaking down each subtarget, focusing on the small steps needed to complete each in easily confrontable gradients. All these subtargets lead to a finished product. You almost can't screw it up. There's no multitasking involved, just one simple step—one simple action—after the other for you to execute. Once each action is complete, you move to the next action and complete that. All of these actions lead to a finished LEGO product. At the end, it's pretty amazing what you can build by simply completing these easy subtargets one at a time.

Now, let's imagine for a second that you put this level of engineering into your company. In terms of goals or targets for the company, most set them with good intentions of hitting them, but unfortunately good intentions aren't enough. You have to know exactly what the goals and targets (end product) are and then you have to work each one back to break them down into simple subtargets that can be easily explained and executed by you or your team. By doing this, you can remove time to attain a goal and ensure that it actually is attained. In my opinion, most targets are missed simply because they were never broken down into a LEGO type of instructions with subtargets that can be easily executed. It takes some time and work to break down targets to this level, but it will save a whole lot of frustration and headaches that come from missed targets or taking far too long to hit a target.

Look through all aspects of your company and dissect immediate goals to take the time to break down each goal into small subtargets that lead toward the goal. Keep breaking each target down until it can't be reduced any further. Although LEGO is for children, the workability is brilliant and should be applied to companies across the board. People have a tendency to make things entirely too complex and sophisticated in this day and age. As the saying goes, "Don't reinvent the wheel." Use what is successful 100 percent of the time. Heck, go buy LEGOs if you have to and study the instructions to understand how they do it. I know I have (hundreds of them in fact—I have a five-year-old!) and every time I build a new LEGO, I think about how smart LEGO's project management was. No one does it like LEGO.

Why You're Unique

Although competition is a popular topic in business, it's truly an overrated one. Take a look at it from this angle: Have you ever met anyone just like you? Exactly like you? I doubt it. How about your thoughts? Ideas? Do you feel those are pretty unique? Do you think there is anyone else in the world with the exact thoughts and ideas with the same twists and character? No, I don't either. I have never met two people exactly the same . . . ever. Nor have I come across two companies exactly the same. Heck, two companies could produce the exact same product or service in the exact same city, and they would most definitely be different. Human nature makes them different. All of the people, personalities, ideas, thoughts, and human creation make them different. So why are you ever worried about competition? Just focus on being you and doing what you do. Focus on delivering your product or service to your clients the way you feel it would work best. Damn the other similar companies. Let them play their game; you play yours.

The idea of competition is just that: an idea. It's propaganda that was injected into the global economy. I'm sure it was done for someone's gain, but it doesn't help you or me. You simply need to refine your craft, be unique, improve your services, and train and challenge your people to help them reach their potential. Business is like playing golf. The only competition in golf is mastering the course to beat your last score or your best score. Focus on playing better in your own company. Beat last week's numbers and improve your game consistently. Wasting time learning and finding out what the "competition" is doing is just that—a waste of time. Not only does it waste your time, it also infects your uniqueness so you start taking on the competition's style rather than being yourself. As you watch and learn what your competition is doing, you start to become them. This will hurt your overall company and culture. Don't invalidate yourself to think that somehow your competition knows better than you do or can come up with better ideas than you can. It's absurd. Keep your mind fresh, come up with your own ideas, and infuse them into your company. I may be the first to tell you this, but you need to hear it: you're unique!

Don't Get Too Serious

As we grow a little older and become more involved in business, which includes the ups and downs that sometimes occur, it's easy to get a little too serious about it all. We tend to become a little edgier with people. A little less polite at times. A little less friendly. All the while, we're working toward being successful, but the irony is that being serious is very counterproductive to success.

Richard Branson is someone I admire in business. If you know a little about him, then you know that he's not remotely serious about his work and yet his successes are enormous both financially and generally. One could argue that he has a lot to be happy about and that's true, but he's been this way all along. If you inspect the points in your life that worked out the best—the times when everything seemed to go your way—I'm willing to bet that it was the time when you were having the most fun and were playful in spirit.

Monitor your level of seriousness and focus on making yourself act and be less serious; you'll see greater success when you do. You can always be determined and professional and focused on what you're doing, but keep a light heart and have fun with it—because if you're not having fun, you may as well get out now.

Genuine Interest and Care

Many salespeople try too hard to sell by doing all the talking and essentially pitching their product or service in a sales-y way, but this isn't needed to sell. In fact, it adds unnecessary effort to the sales process because most people are naturally skeptical of someone trying to sell something, especially someone trying too hard to sell something.

So the next time you're in a sales meeting or on a call, focus on being genuinely interested. In other words, really care and ask questions about the other person's company and service or product. Ask "why" questions and work to *help* the client figure out the problem that needs to be solved. View the situation from the client's eyes, not your own. Act as if you work for that company and have been tasked with the job to correct or handle the specific problem you're discussing. Work as a team with your prospect to figure out the very best decision for the company and to determine whether the product or service you're selling is the right fit. Do all this and the chance of you selling and closing the deal will be fantastically high.

The funny thing about selling this way is that there isn't much selling that goes on. The prospects will typically sell themselves and say something like, "What do we need to do to get started?" That's when you know that you've done it correctly. Sales will become less "effort-y" with this approach.

Damn the Torpedoes . . . They'll Swerve First

Too often in business, "risk" is a topic of discussion that dictates decisions and actions. Although every company has to be responsible and smart about the actions it takes, it's important to recognize that risk is a very subjective concept. One may think starting a company is risky simply because he or she doesn't personally know much about starting a company. Anything you don't completely know about tends to contain an element of fear. But, on the other hand, someone who is highly educated, has the knowledge of what it takes to start a company, and is a competent entrepreneur will not consider starting a company risky. So "risk" is very subjective. Everything relies on how well you're trained, how much knowledge you have, your confidence, and finally your competence to take calculated actions that lead to a postulated outcome.

Once you're armed with the correct information, you've been trained, and you know how to do what you're doing, then damn the torpedoes—go full steam ahead. Do not waver. Be aggressive and push your boundaries toward zones of discomfort so that you'll make a new "comfortable" for yourself. Push yourself to the next stage. Don't kid yourself; you will get push back from those on your team. People will doubt your decisions. Don't take offense and don't fall into agreement with what they're saying; forge ahead and see whatever it is that you've decided to do through to completion. Your intention and forward thrust combined with your certainty in what you're doing will result in the outcome you have decided on, and the barriers will move out of the way or be stampeded as you go. Inertia is your friend; use it. Plan, yes. Prepare, yes. Study, train, lay out the correct actions, and then do it with the throttle fully slammed forward. I promise you, the torpedoes will get out of the way.

Money Motivation and Caring about What You Do with Passion

I'm fully aware that every company ultimately needs to make money and thereby a profit. That's blatantly obvious. But all too often I see businesspeople and friends doing something for money. They actually start with money in mind. It's a terrible business plan, and it's stupid. If you're trying to figure out how to make money, don't start by trying to come up with a way to make money. Sorry, but the world isn't rigged that way. I'm shocked at how many people, trying to come up with something that will make them money, are surprised when it doesn't work out and they fail miserably. This isn't opinion. This is a physical truth of the world we live in. But you don't have to take my word for it; you can always try it and see for yourself.

The only way to approach a business or idea that you want to launch is to start with the why. Why does that thing make you excited? Why do you care? Are you passionate about it? Are you so addicted to the concept of it that you get excited and energized just thinking about the future of it? If so, you're on track. You can always take a second to imagine your business idea or a new idea for your current company, and when envisioning what it could be, if you start to get excited then it's something that has legs. That personal care about what you're doing creates energy. That energy will convert into forward motion. It's contagious and will affect everyone around you in a positive way. Build your company with that energy.

Put care into everything that you do, including how you handle your clients' companies and how you service them. Care with passion and drive that concept into your people's minds. It's sheer magic. You can move mountains with this. Get any money motivation out of the environment and out of the minds of the people you work with. This isn't to say don't think about money; you have to make money, and you have to be profitable. But you don't have to be motivated by it. Money motivations will lead to crappy products and services, unethical practices, and other undesirable conditions.

Conversely, care and passion will unequivocally lead to incredible products and services and great people, and they will drive people to want to come work for you and new companies to want to work with you. It's a powerful and contagious operating basis. It's not necessarily something that is maintained by itself, though. You have to drum up that emotion every day.

Keep a close eye on what you care about, that is, what gets you excited, and flow that energy throughout the company. We have signs on our walls that clearly state why we do what we do and what we care about so that our people can see it and read it every day in multiple locations. When this concept starts to fade for people, we walk them over to a sign and have them read it to remind them who we are and why we do what we do. We handle any barriers they're running into or any situation that caused them to become unclear on this. We've found that this exercise reinvigorates our people, charging them up to go back and deliver what we've written on our walls. People operate this way. They love to do something for a purpose and do something that they care about. Money will take someone only so far, and it will not maintain motivation. It's like using sugar for your source of energy. It may spike your energy for 30 minutes, but then you'll crash; it can't be sustained. A diet balanced in high-energy organic foods combined with exercise, sleep, and vitamins, on the other hand, will help you sustain that energy long term. This is similar to what care and passion do in a company. It's like a high-energy diet for the minds of your people and yourself. Try and you'll see the difference.

Know Who You Are

This sounds simple enough, but the truth is, a company is like a person. A company has a personality, and you need to define what it stands for. What's the goal? What's the purpose of what you're doing? It all starts here. You need to know with complete clarity who you are as a company and what you stand for. This should motivate every single decision and action in the company.

There's a saying that goes, "If you don't know where you're going, any road will take you there." You need to define why you exist as a company; from there, you can set targets and make future goals accordingly.

For us, knowing our goal was the turning point of our agency. We clearly defined the goal and purpose and then posted it on our walls. We drilled our staff so they knew it. We put it in every training pack for our people to study. When anyone in our company gets derailed and performance suffers, we start by getting that person back on our goal and purpose.

For example, we had a sales rep who was going through the motions of selling and working to close sales but with very little or no results. She didn't understand why she was doing what she was doing, so it became a situation where she was just selling to sell. We reviewed the goal and basic purpose and discussed how it applied and why. We reviewed why we are doing what we do and how it affects our clients' companies. She injected that purpose—why we exist—into her sales process. The results were terrific. Her statistics immediately improved, and she felt better about selling. Without a clear goal and purpose, a lot of people just go to work and go through the motions to get a paycheck, only to do it all over again the next day. That isn't the type of company you should be striving to build.

You need to know why you exist and what you do—and so do your people. It can't be just words on the wall either; it needs to be a living philosophy within your group that is reiterated every single day. This will move mountains for your company.

Push Yourself

It's pretty easy to coast in life because although most people want to attain their goals, many don't actually want the extra headache involved in making it happen. The additional amount of work is significant, no two ways about it. But know this, to attain success or any goal it requires only that you push yourself a little more than you are now. The funny thing is that most people don't push themselves very hard at all. They just sort of do what is necessary. This means that if you're one of the few who pushes yourself harder than most, the chances of success or attaining any given goal is quite good.

Just look at any goal you're trying to attain and write down what you think you would do to attain it or what would be normal for you and then step everything up a notch.

Using fitness as an example, say you want to attain a certain physique. You think you will need to run 1 mile three times per week to attain your fitness goal. Write down your plan, but instead of writing that you'll run 1 mile three times a week, write that you will run 2 miles four times each week. Yes, it's added work and it requires you to push yourself relatively hard, but you have to ask yourself, "How badly do you actually want to get in shape?"

By doing this exercise, you may find that (1) you really want to attain the goal and are willing to push yourself to do what it takes to get it or (2) you don't really want it bad enough and so you settle with the idea that you won't ever attain it. I use running and getting in shape as an example because it has a great correlation to business and success in general. It takes physical effort to attain anything, and you need to assess what you're willing to do and how badly you actually want the goal you've named because it will play a key role in how much you push yourself to attain it. It's also not a one-time thing. You're not going to decide once, and then all is good. You need to decide and then remind yourself every single day, every hour, why you are doing it and what you want to stay motivated to keep pushing yourself. You're the best personal coach you could have. You need to push yourself because no one else will.

Conclusion

Ultimately, everything in this book is completely useless unless you use it. It needs to be applied to work. That's the biggest takeaway I can offer. Focus on application. Focus on execution. Focus on your goals. These are lessons I have learned—sometimes the hard way. Stay *focused* and take one point at a time and put it into your company. Then take the next point and put that in. Be methodical. It's easy to become distracted by the day-to-day hectic nature of business, but you need to be disciplined to make a distinct plan for each and every day and have clear objectives to accomplish for that day.

Put these points in one by one, and you will see results bit by bit. As the saying goes, "Rome wasn't built in a day." So set goals that are long term and then visualize the long-term outcome and take tactical daily measures to work toward attaining those goals.

Ultimately, you will look up and realize that you are attaining your goals and the company is better than it was. For us, we measure everything using statistics that measure production and display the results as line graphs on a wall; this allows us to monitor and see week to week how we're doing. It's critical to measure how well you're doing in a way that makes it possible for you to predict outcomes both good and bad so you can correct or push what is working as needed and you can also course correct as necessary. We also use programs and projects that we type up with clear objectives and targets that are listed out to align with hitting those goals. So, to clarify, we set a goal and then add that to the top of our program or project and below it we define each action step or target that needs to be executed in order to attain the goal. Think of it like this: if you bought a new bookshelf from the store which required assembly, it would come with instructions with step-by-step actions that would be needed to actually build the bookshelf. You should view your goals the same way. It would be quite silly to buy a bookshelf that requires assembly with no instructions and the chances of it being put together properly with all the parts are slim. For us, attaining a goal is very transparent. We can see that our statistics have increased, and we can see that the specific targets we set have been executed. This is key. You want to make progress transparent. You need to be able to measure it and see progress.

Goals need to be attainable so that you can execute targets and attain the goals. Don't set lofty or vague goals such as "grow the company"; these types of goals waste a lot of time and spin everyone into a chaotic confused state while they move in different directions trying to attain them. Set specific goals such as, "Build our sales team to 25 reps to attain our gross income goals"; then break down the required steps to achieve that goal into smaller subgoals. That's the real difference between success and failure: the ability to clearly articulate simple doable goals and targets that you need to accomplish and then the successful execution of those targets. If you work out the goals and targets in a clear fashion, knowing whether or not you're making progress is not an issue. It does take focus. It does take dedication to constantly push yourself and others forward to attain the goals set out, but always ask yourself why you're doing this. What's your purpose? Remind yourself of that every day and push yourself with that in mind.

The points in this book will help you get there faster and will help steer you into safe waters, but at the end of the day, you have to be the driving force of your company to make things happen.

The overall success of your company is entirely up to you. The external factors of the world have nothing to do with it. It all comes down to whether you applied the right steps and made them happen or not. Knowing that should be a relief to you. It means that when you wake up every morning, the fate of your company is entirely in your hands.

The only thing that can stop you is you. So if you stay out of your own way, take the lessons from this book, and diligently work daily on the tactical steps to get there—you will.

Acknowledgments

To say it was all Wil and myself who made this book happen would be a gross misrepresentation of how success is really built. We have amazing people around us who are loyal and trustworthy and can get the show on the road for whom we are truly thankful. Success is composed of many different people in our lives who contribute to the effort and we would like to deeply express our appreciation and admiration to those people. We want to thank our families for supporting us along the way, our amazing staff that we honestly couldn't have succeeded without, our clients whom we find fantastically interesting and who pose a challenge for us every day—figuring out the best ways to help them grow, which in turn helps us become better. Our children, who push us to create a better future, our publisher who has been so helpful and pleasant to work with, and a special thanks to Scott

Schaefer who helped arrange the book and bring it all together to make a fantastic final version.

Additionally, we would like to thank those who have actively helped us along the way or inspired us to become better:

Grant Cardone
Jack Dorsey
Gwain Cornish
Richard Branson
Mark H. McCormack
David Ogilvy
Gurbaksh Chahal
Tony Hsieh
Jason Fried
Will Smith
Howard Schultz
Steve Jobs
Elon Musk
Scott Harrison
Nelson Mandela
Susan Davis
John Fish
Bud Reichel
Ibonne Demogines
Jefferson Davis
Walt Disney

About the Authors

Robert Cornish

I've been fascinated with business as long as I can remember. I've wanted to be an entrepreneur most of my life and closely followed other entrepreneurs I admire. Over the years I have constantly studied the successful patterns of people and companies that have made it and set the pace. I've implemented those successes into my own life and then developed my own through various ventures. Ultimately, as you go, the picture becomes clearer and it gets easier and easier to see the next steps. I founded Richter10.2 Media Group with my partner Wil Seabrook in March 2008. Today the company employs nearly 60 people on staff with thousands of clients around the globe. I have been featured in such publications as *Bloomberg Businessweek* and *Selling Power*.

I grew up following and watching the growth of a plastics company that my father played a major role in as a senior executive, one that grew from $1 million in revenue to a publicly traded company on the New York Stock Exchange with more than $2 billion in annual revenues—all in the span of about 10 years. The observations and lessons associated with this experience, discussing business ideas or overhearing my father talk about business while in social meetings, helped shape the way I thought about business and how I approach my own company strategies.

I have started four companies since 2002, and two have attained $1 million in revenue in less than 3 years. For as long as I can remember, I have had a passion for business and entrepreneurship, which has driven me to work toward creating great companies. My focus has always been on the actual mechanics of a company. How it ticks. What makes it operational and the best practices associated with making it run better to allow it to expand and push through any and all barriers that arise. At the age of 28, with my partner, no investment capital of any kind, two desks, phones, and computers, I founded an agency to help other companies grow and flourish; this company has now become one of the fastest growing companies in America.

Wil Seabrook

How do you measure success? The answer is probably unique to every individual. As a culture, particularly in the United States, we tend to value material wealth and extraordinary accomplishments. I have been fortunate enough to achieve some unusual successes. I spent most of my twenties chasing after a major label recording contract as a singer and musician and accomplished my goals in 2002 by signing deals with Maverick/Warner Brothers as well as signing a publishing contract for my songwriting skills with Warner/Chappell Music.

I have heard my songs on the radio all over the United States, the United Kingdom, Europe, and elsewhere. I have had my music featured in TV shows from *Dawson's Creek* and *ER* to *Boston Legal, Jersey Shore,* and many others. I have shared the stage with world-class acts and performed for 20,000 people live and 20 million people on international TV. I've recorded at Capitol Records Studio B, where Frank Sinatra and other artists recorded some of the most enduring music of our time.

Despite these successes, there was one key ingredient that was missing that left me feeling overwhelmed and miserable at a time when I should have been reveling at a level of success rarely achieved by those who aspire to it. That ingredient was know-how. As a capable communicator and an incredibly stubborn, hardworking person, I have always had the ability to come up with creative ideas and then work like the devil to bring them to fruition in the real world. What I never had before my partnership with Robert and our work at Richter10.2 was a workable system of how to organize and administrate the projects I was so busy creating out of thin air.

Without having workable systems with which to keep the plates spinning and the machine growing, I would inevitably build a great-looking house of cards, only to have the slightest breeze knock it over at the worst possible time. I have seen so many able, well-intentioned executives, from start-ups to Fortune 500 companies, drowning under the weight of carrying an entire organization on their backs day in and day out.

Robert and I began with a handshake agreement to create the kind of company that we'd both be excited to work for, whether we were answering fans or running the whole show. We've succeeded by keeping everything as simple as we possibly can and by constantly remembering that at the end of the day, it's all about the people involved: employees, contractors, clients, and their customers. When we look at adopting policy or a new way of doing things, we ask one simple question: Does this work? In other words, does this create the desired outcome as simply and efficiently as possible? If the answer is yes, then we keep it. If the answer is no, then no matter how fun or exciting or "bright" an idea seems, we push it aside and keep our focus on our long-term goals.

I have had some of the most amazing experiences one could hope for professionally as a musician. But I've never felt the sense of confidence, certainty, and excitement about the future that I do now because I know with total certainty that not only do I have ideas that are workable and helpful to myself and others but I also have the tools I need to make those ideas a long-term, stable reality for myself and the people I care about.

Happiness is not achieving your goals; it's enjoying the process of getting there. At Richter10.2 we focus on the process every day, and I've enjoyed the journey every step of the way.

Richter10.2 Media Group
www.richter10point2.com
E-mail: info@richter10point2.com